Epistle
to the
Son
of
the Wolf

D1059598

Epistle
to the
Son
of
the Wolf

by Bahá'u'lláh

Translated
by
Shoghi Effendi

BAHÁ'Í PUBLISHING TRUST
WILMETTE, ILLINOIS 60091

Bahá'í Publishing Trust, Wilmette, IL 60091

Library of Congress Cataloging-in-Publication Data

Bahá' Alláh, 1817–1892.
Epistle to the Son of the Wolf.

Translation of: Lawḥ-i Ibn Ẕi'b.
Bibliography: p.
Includes index.
1. Bahai Faith.   I.   Title.
BP360.B68413   1988   297'.8982   87-35141
ISBN 0-87743-048-9
ISBN 0-87743-235-X (pocket size ed.)

*Epistle
to the
Son
of
the Wolf*

INTRODUCTION

"I was walking in the Land of Ṭá (Ṭihrán)—the dayspring of the signs of thy Lord—when lo, I heard the lamentation of the pulpits and the voice of their supplication unto God, blessed and glorified be He. They cried out and said: 'O God of the world and Lord of the nations! Thou beholdest our state and the things which have befallen us....'"

We, the two billion people currently on the planet, are living at a time when not only the pulpits of all the religions, but all things must be condemning us, each in that voice which, according to the Qur'án, God has given to all things: "God, Who giveth a voice to all things, hath given us a voice...." (41:20). We who have killed some forty-five million human beings in the past thirty-five years, strangers whom we did not even know by name. We who have denied our qualitative difference from the animals and have tried to live in their world, an attempt which has proved as successful as would be the animal's to turn into a tree or the tree's to be a stone. We who spend our time devising elaborate excuses to justify our ways; who always blame someone else, who always want someone else to save us.

It is not surprising that Bahá'u'lláh, the Persian nobleman Who declared His spiritual mission in 1863, should also say: "... *ye walk on My earth complacent*

i

and self-satisfied, heedless that My earth is weary of you and everything within it shunneth you."

Meanwhile we long for happiness, and then reject it when it is brought to us. Because happiness for human beings means being raised out of the blind physical world into the conscious life of the spirit, and this can only be done by the Prophet of God. At His advent we fight Him and resist Him, whether He is Moses or Buddha, Jesus or Muḥammad, or Bahá'u'lláh.

Man is showing by his acts that he has lost God and in consequence has also lost himself. "And be ye not like those," the Qur'án warns, "who forget God, and whom He hath therefore caused to forget their own selves." (59:19). Man is bewildered—straying in a wilderness. He must find the meaning in the universe again, and this meaning is God as expressed by the Prophet; then he will rediscover his own self, the reflection of the meaning; then he will have a way of life in keeping with the facts and will consciously follow it.

A seventeen year old boy is referred to in this book. He was a troublesome youth and his father was worried about him. Then Bahá'u'lláh, imprisoned in the barracks at 'Akká, summoned him. Following their interview, the boy, alone and on foot, carried to Persia Bahá'u'lláh's Tablet to the Sháh. He reached the capital after a four months' journey; he fasted, prayed, and waited on a rock until he saw the Sháh and his suite going hunting in the direction of the hill villages north of Ṭihrán. He approached them and called out in

Arabic: "O King! I have come to thee from Sheba with a weighty message." (This is what the lapwing said to Solomon when it returned from seeing Balkis on her golden throne: Qur'án 27:22.) The Tablet was taken from the boy and delivered to the priests. They read it, and recommended that the boy be put to death. The executioners branded him with hot irons for three days; a photograph, taken of him under torture, is extant. Then they beat his head to a pulp with a rifle butt and threw his body down a hole.

Bahá'u'lláh wrote, in a Tablet to the boy's father—Ḥájí 'Abdu'l-Majíd, who himself was to suffer martyrdom later on in Khurásán: *"Dost thou think that he is dead? No, by the Revealer of Signs! Through him the spirit of life joyfully moveth in the hearts of the universe."* In this same Tablet, Bahá'u'lláh says that in Badí' *"the spirit of might and power was breathed"*; that he was created anew; that he smiled, and *"should We have commanded him, he would have subdued all in heaven and upon the earth."* That *"Joy overtook him,"* and that he went to his death *"with power and authority, advancing with such strength as to overturn the Supreme Concourse and the denizens of the Cities of Names."*

The point is that Badí' was recreated. He was in Bible terminology born again. He saw the truth and died as a sacrifice to it. Those who believe in Bahá'u'lláh today are seldom called to join the ranks of the more than 20,000 who gave up their lives in the Heroic Age of His Cause—who, as the present text states, *"threw down the precious crown of life for the sake of Him Who is the Incomparable Friend."* But they are repeatedly obliged to disregard their own likes and dislikes, to discipline their conduct, to win a victory over their own selves—a process longer, less spectacular, and perhaps more painful than martyrdom.

It is only through such a process that the planet can be made habitable again: that human beings, motivated by love, will voluntarily begin to act in ways that are worthy of the nature of man. Bahá'u'lláh writes in the *Hidden Words*, *"I created thee rich, why dost thou bring thyself down to poverty? Noble I made thee, wherewith dost thou abase thyself?"*

1.

The thinking world has caught up, by now, with the basic teachings which Bahá'u'lláh (1817–1892) enunciated more than seventy years ago. Today no enlightened mind can disagree with such Bahá'í fundamentals as these: "The oneness and wholeness of the human race." (This is the most vital of them all, the establishment of this principle being the central purpose of the Bahá'í Faith. The unification of mankind is, Bahá'u'lláh says, inevitable, and marks the last stage in the evolution of man toward maturity.) Service to humanity the worthiest of all endeavors. Religion, *"the chief instrument of the establishment of order in the world,"* to be taught to children in all schools in such a way as not to produce fanaticism or prejudice. All religions are essentially one, differing in their outer aspects only because they appeared at different periods in history and thus addressed themselves to varying situations. The reconciliation of religion and science, which are the two most powerful forces in human life. Education available to all. Equal opportunities for both sexes, equality for women being directly linked to world peace. A world federal system, reduction in national armaments, collective security. The adoption of an international auxiliary language and script. Work for all.

Bahá'u'lláh states that justice is *"the best beloved of all things,"* and its advent inevitable. That consultation, frank and unfettered, is *"the bestower of understanding,"* and the bedrock of His Order. That the acquisition of knowledge is incumbent on everyone, *"arts, crafts and sciences"* being extolled. That wealth gained through crafts and professions is praiseworthy. That poverty will disappear, as will exorbitant wealth. That the trustees of the "House of Justice" are to legislate on all matters not expressly set forth in Bahá'í writings (this international Bahá'í body is empowered to rescind its previous legislation and to incorporate into its machinery whatever is considered necessary to keep the Faith "in the forefront of all progressive movements."). Constitutional government, combining "the ideals of republicanism and the majesty of kingship" is recommended. Agriculture is to be given special regard. The press is specifically extolled, newspapers being described as *"the mirror of the world"* and those responsible for their production directed to free themselves from "malice, passion, and prejudice, to be just and fair-minded, to be painstaking in their inquiries and ascertain all the facts in every situation." Bahá'u'lláh further reemphasizes the ban on the waging of holy war and the destruction of books; requires of His followers that they obey the Government of the country in which they live; and singles out for special praise individuals of learning and wisdom whom He describes as "*eyes*" to the body of mankind.*

What the world does not yet guess at is the capacity of Bahá'u'lláh's projected world order, functioning in the universal recognition of one God, to "re-create society." The world community is His primary concern. Religion has often, in the past, produced the good individual. The primary object of Bahá'u'lláh's religion is to produce the good society. His administrative system offers, Bahá'ís believe, the only satisfactory arrangement between individual and community, between free will and authority, equilibrating the prerogatives of each.

This balance will have to be created if humanity is to develop an age of peace. We have seen the dictator state crushing out the individual, and we have seen lynch law flouting the group. The point has been debated down the ages. Rúmí the mystic begs God to deliver him from his free will, a burden which he says even heaven and the angels refused, and only man accepted; he compares himself to a camel with pack

---

* Cf. Shoghi Effendi, *God Passes By*, p. 216 ff., *The Unfoldment of World Civilization*, etc.

sores, whose panniers sag first on one side and then on the other, and asks that the ill-balanced load be taken from him, and that instead he be made to roll here and there like a polo ball. In contrast with such a view was the way of life in Calvin's Geneva, where according to laws regulating inns, no one was permitted "to sit up after nine o'clock at night, except spies."

When the balance between the person and society finally obtains we shall know that man has begun his maturity. Obviously, both individual and group will have to give up something of what they now have, just as the nations will have to yield some of their present sovereignty in favor of the world commonwealth, but this will prove no more of a hardship than the sacrifice of bait to catch fish.

2.

Here is a world religion to match the new world. It has no priesthood; it accepts no funds except from registered adherents. It has solved the problems of successorship, administration and schism, factors which virtually destroyed, almost at their inception, the unity of all previous faiths. In this case Bahá'u'lláh the Founder Himself designated in His written Covenant that His eldest son 'Abdu'l-Bahá was His authorized Successor and Interpreter. 'Abdu'l-Bahá in His own Will and Testament appointed as Guardian and Interpreter His grandson Shoghi Effendi, who in turn is to appoint the next Guardian, the written appointment to be ratified by vote of a council of "Hands of the Cause." The democratically-elected institutions which in conjunction with the Guardian administer the Faith were likewise stipulated in the writings of the Founder. The present task of Bahá'ís the world over is two-fold, involving both consolidation in studying the Teachings and practicing the Bahá'í way of life—and expansion: presenting this Faith to the public for free investigation. Bahá'í communities are now to be found in more than one hundred countries around the globe.

Study of the writings is a lifetime occupation. Although the tenets of the Faith are readily grasped, the Teachings are vast, disclosing new horizons as the individual's experience develops. It is far from true that all Bahá'ís are intellectuals—there are communities of Persian villagers—but it is certain that the Teachings themselves and the effort to bring them before the public act as a strong incentive to acquire diversified knowledge. 'Abdu'l-Bahá writes, "The dominion of kings has an ending . . . but the sovereignty of science is everlasting. . . ." and again, "All blessings are divine in origin but none can be compared with this power of intellectual investigation and research which is an eternal gift producing fruits of unending delight . . . All other blessings are temporary; this is an everlasting possession."

3.

Bahá'u'lláh wrote a hundred books. They consist of laws, principles, and exhortations; of warnings and prophecies; of prayers and meditations; of commentaries, interpretations, discourses, and homilies; of the proclamation of His mission to kings, ministers, and ecclesiastics of both East and West; of writings addressed specifically to leaders in intellectual, political, literary, mystical, commercial and humanitarian fields. His last major Tablet is this present book. It was revealed about one year before His death in 1892.

Some three months after this text was finished, Bahá'u'lláh expressed His wish to leave the world. He was now living, still an exile and prisoner as He had been, here and there throughout the Middle East, for the previous forty years, in the Mansion of Bahjí outside 'Akká. From this time on it became clear from the tone of His remarks, although He made no open reference to it, that the end of His life on earth was approaching. Years before, He had described in His Tablet of the Vision—revealed on the anniversary of His Forerunner and Prophet-Herald, the martyred Báb—how the white-clad *"Luminous Maid"* had appeared before Him and urged Him to hasten to His *"other dominions,"* dominions *"whereon the eyes of the people of names have never fallen."* Now a few more months passed, until after a brief illness He died at dawn, on May 29, 1892, in the seventy-fifth year of His age.

Then the famous telegram was sent to Sulṭán 'Abdu'l-Ḥamíd, whose prisoner He had been. It began with the words: "The Sun of Bahá has set." Then mourners from 'Akká and the neighboring villages crowded the fields around the Mansion, and notables of the Shí'ih and Sunní, Christian, Jewish and Druse communities, poets, divines and officials, from cities as far away as Damascus, Aleppo, Beirut and Cairo, sent their written tributes to Him, and Nabíl the historian could not be consoled and drowned himself in the Mediterranean Sea.

This book has therefore a special place in the hierarchy of all Bahá'u'lláh's books. It is the last one. It is besides, a kind of anthology, and one particularly valuable, the material having been selected by the Author Himself. It includes some of the best-known and most characteristic of His writings, as well as proofs establishing the validity of His Cause.

4.

There were two brothers in Iṣfahán, men of wealth, widely known for their philanthropies and the excellence of their character. The head priest, Mír Muḥammad-Ḥusayn, the cleric whose function it was to recite the prayers in the Friday mosque, owed them a large sum of money. To evade the debt, he denounced them as followers of the Báb. He knew exactly what this would mean. Their beautiful houses were at once given over to the mob and stripped, and even the trees and flowers in their gardens were torn away. Whatever they had was taken. Then Shaykh Muḥammad-Báqir, whom Bahá'u'lláh names "The Wolf," pronounced their death sentence. The Prince-Governor, Ẓillu's-Sulṭán, eldest son of the Sháh, ratified it. The brothers were chained. Their heads were severed. Their bodies were dragged to the great open square of the city, and there they were exposed to every indignity the mob could inflict. *"In such wise,"* 'Abdu'l-Bahá has written, *"was the blood of these two brothers shed that the Christian priest of Julfa cried out, lamented and wept on that day."*

Afterward "The Wolf," whom Bahá'u'lláh condemned in His Lawḥ-i-Burhán ("Tablet of the Proof") and called *"the last trace of sunlight upon the mountain-top,"* saw the steady decline of his prestige and died miserably, in acute remorse. As for his accomplice Mír Muḥammad-Ḥusayn, Bahá'u'lláh stigmatized him as the "She-Serpent," and declared him to be *"infinitely more wicked than the oppressor of Karbilá."* This man was expelled from Iṣfahán, wandered from one village to another, and finally sickened and died of a disease so foul-smelling that his own wife and daughter could not bear to attend him.

Years later the Governor, Zillu's-Sulṭán, was exiled to Geneva. In 1911 when 'Abdu'l-Bahá was at Thonon, staying at the Hôtel du Parc, Zillu's-Sulṭán came there. Hippolyte Dreyfus, distinguished scholar and traveler, the first French Bahá'í, had met him in Persia, visiting him in his tent when the prince was on a hunting trip. Now he saw him again, on the terrace of the hotel. M. Dreyfus described the meeting to Juliet Thompson, who arrived the following day, and she has recorded it in her diary: "The Master too was on the terrace, pacing up and down at a little distance. Hippolyte was standing in the doorway when he saw Zillu's-Sulṭán coming up the steps. The prince approached and greeted him, then turned a startled look toward the Master. 'Who is that Persian nobleman?' he asked. 'That,' answered Hippolyte, 'is 'Abdu'l-Bahá.' And now Z̤illu's-Sulṭán spoke very humbly. 'Take me to Him,' he begged. Hippolyte told me all about it. 'If you could have seen the brute, Juliet, mumbling out his miserable excuses! But the Master took him in His arms and said, 'All those things are in the past. Never think of them again.' "

The two brothers who were put to death by "The Wolf" and his accomplice are known to Bahá'ís as the King of Martyrs and the Beloved of Martyrs. They are also referred to as the Twin Shining Lights. Their names were Mírzá Muḥammad-Ḥasan and Mírzá Muḥammad-Ḥusayn, and they were siyyids—descendants of the Prophet Muḥammad. In after years a special link associated them with the West, because in 1933 the American Keith Ransom-Kehler, representing her country's National Bahá'í Assembly, visited their graves and placed flowers there. Not many days afterward she fell ill of smallpox and died, and her body was brought back and laid in the neighborhood of theirs.

This present book is addressed to the son of the man who murdered the Twin Shining Lights, the Son of the Wolf. He was called S͟hayk͟h Muḥammad Taqíy-i-Najafí. A Muslim cleric of Iṣfahán, he and his pupils kicked and trampled the corpse of Mírzá As͟hraf, still another Bahá'í who, in 1888, was killed by order of the mullás of that city. He is often addressed in this text as "O S͟hayk͟h!"—this being a title denoting a

chief, prelate or man of learning. Other persons are
also called upon in the course of the work; the people
of the Bayán—those followers of the Báb who failed
to recognize Bahá'u'lláh, reminiscent of those followers of John the Baptist who failed to acknowledge
Jesus Christ, are addressed. And Hádí, a religious
leader terrified of losing his rank when he was called a
disciple of the Báb, and who tried to destroy every
copy of the Bayán, the Báb's great book. And the
Wolf himself, in passages quoted from the "Tablet of
the Proof," and Queen Victoria and Napoleon III and
others, in quoted passages. Although the Tablet is primarily directed to the Son of the Wolf he seems almost
incidental; Bahá'u'lláh is, rather, speaking beyond
him to all humanity.

Some of the terminology will be familiar only to
students of Islámics, for the Bahá'í Faith comes out
of Islám as Christianity comes out of Judaism. For
example the Arabic verse on p. 17 contrasts the Sanctuary (Ḥaram), the sacred place where no blood may
be shed, with the place outside the Sanctuary (Ḥill)
where the shedding of blood is not unlawful, and refers
to Bahá'u'lláh's willingness to sacrifice His life any-
where and under any conditions. Or there is reference
to the Sadratu'l-Muntahá. This is the "Divine Lote-
Tree," the "Sidrah Tree, which marks the boundary,"
the "Lote-Tree of the extremity," the "Tree beyond
which neither men nor angels can pass," and which
stands in the Seventh Heaven, the highest Paradise, at
the right hand of the Throne of God. Reference to it

occurs obliquely in Qur'án 53:9 and directly in 53:14, and the two visions there described are traditionally related to Muḥammad's Vision of the Ascension or Mi'ráj (cf. Súrih 17:1). In Bahá'í writings this Tree symbolizes the Prophet or Manifestation of God.

The Mother-Book is referred to in Qur'án 43:3; Rodwell translates this as "the archetypal Book" and comments, "the Mother of the Book, i.e. the original of the Koran, preserved before God." Sale says, "the preserved table; which is the original of all the scriptures in general." To Bahá'ís the Mother Book, or Preserved Tablet, or Guarded Tablet, means the Word of God, the Manifestation of God in every age, or His Book.

The Súrih of Tawḥíd, called "The Unity," is Súrih 112 of the Qur'án.

"Name" sometimes means the Prophet or Manifestation of God. On p. 58 we read, "Be thou not of them who called upon God by one of His names, but who, when He Who is the object of all names appeared, denied Him and turned aside from Him . . ."

The Aqṣá Mosque is the Temple that is "most remote." It is built on the site of Solomon's Temple at Jerusalem.

On p. 73 there is a play upon words. The martyr cries out that he has kept both Bahá'u'lláh and the blood money; Bahá in Arabic means glory, in Persian value.

Balál, great, early believer in Muḥammad, was an Ethiopian slave. Cruelly tortured by the idolatrous

Meccans, he refused to recant his faith in Islám. Later he was freed, and although he stammered Muḥammad appointed him the first muezzin. The reference on p. 76 is to the fact that because of his affliction he pronounced the letters "sh" as "s."

"Remnant of the Prophet" on p. 80 refers to the fact that the martyred brothers were descendants of Muḥammad.

To "rend the Veil of Divinity," p. 83, means to perpetrate an act of sacrilege, symbolized by tearing the veil of the tabernacle in which was the Shekinah, —the Dwelling, the Glory of God—emblem of the Divine Presence. The hamstringing of the She-Camel goes back to Qur'án 7:71; 11:67; 54:27, etc. The She-Camel was a sign of God, the proof of the Prophet Ṣáliḥ's mission. The reference again is to an act of blasphemy.

Ishmael, p. 101, refers to Qur'án 37:100. It is the Muslim teaching that the "son" who was sacrificed was Ishmael, not Isaac, the former being Abraham's only son at that time. (Cf. *Gleanings from the Writings of Bahá'u'lláh*, p. 75).

"Verses concerning the Divine Presence," referred to on p. 115 and elsewhere, are numerous in the Qur'án. Among them are these: Súrih 39:69: "And the earth shall shine with the light [núr] of her Lord, and the Book shall be set, and the prophets shall be brought up, and the witnesses . . . and none shall be wronged." 89:22-23: " . . . when the earth shall be crushed with crushing, crushing, And thy Lord

shall come and the angels rank on rank . . . " 83:6:
"The day when mankind shall stand before the Lord
of the worlds." 20:107, 110: "On that day shall men
follow their summoner . . . and low shall be their
voices before the God of Mercy, nor shalt thou hear
aught but the light footfall . . . And humble shall be
their faces before Him that Liveth . . . "

Rawḍih-khání, p. 121, is ritualistic lamentation for
the martyred Imám Ḥusayn. With the new Advent,
the time of mourning was over; as a symbol of this,
Ṭáhirih, the great poetess who became a convert to
the Faith of the Báb, refused to wear the traditional
mourning for Ḥusayn on the anniversary of his
martyrdom, thus openly defying the people of
Karbilá.

Adrianople, p. 132, is in Arabic Adirnih. Every
letter of the Arabic alphabet has a numerical value,
and according to this (abjad) reckoning the words
Adirnih and Mystery (sirr) are equivalent, the Arabic
letters composing each totalling 260.

The language and script referred to on p. 138 were
never communicated to anyone by Bahá'u'lláh.

The Qayyúm-i-Asmá, p. 139, is the Báb's Commentary on the Súrih of Joseph, whose first chapter
was revealed in the presence of Mullá Ḥusayn, on the
night when the Báb declared His mission in Shíráz,
May 22, 1844. Bahá'u'lláh speaks of it in the *Íqán*
as "the first, the greatest and mightiest of all books"
of the Bábí Dispensation.

The Great Announcement, p. 143, refers to Qur'án 78:1-2 and 38:67: an-Nabáu'l-'Azím.

"He maketh the morning darkness," (Amos 4:12-13) on p. 146, refers to the fact that Mírzá Yaḥyá, known as Ṣubḥ-i-Azal—the Morning of Eternity—denied the Manifestation and betrayed Him.

The statement "None knoweth the time . . ." on p. 157 refutes the disbelievers who claimed that the Advent proclaimed by the Báb to be imminent, would take place only in 2,001, a date arrived at by totalling the numerical value of the letters composing the word Mustaghátḥ, assigned by the Báb as the limit of time fixed for the coming of the promised Manifestation. Mustaghátḥ, means "He Who is Invoked."

The martyrdom of the Imám Ḥusayn at Karbilá is described by Gibbon in the *Decline and Fall of the Roman Empire*, Modern Library Edition, III, 125, 127. Dhi'l-Jawshan is Shimr, who killed Ḥusayn, son of 'Alí and grandson of Muḥammad. (p. 158).

On p. 159, "Súrih of the Qur'án" refers to Súrih 109, "Unbelievers," in which Muḥammad refuses to compromise with the idolatrous Meccans.

Siyyid Muḥammad, the Siyyid of Iṣfahán, is the Antichrist of the Baháʼí Revelation. It was he who misled Mírzá Yaḥyá, half-brother of Baháʼuʼlláh. (Cf. *God Passes By*, p. 164, 189, etc.) This reference occurs on pages 164 and 168 of the present text.

The Mawlavís are an order of whirling dervishes, founded by Jalál-i-Dín Rúmí, 1207-1273 A.D. For Khiḍr, a name which means green, see traditions concerning Qur'án, 18:64. In Islám he is the discoverer and custodian of the water of life, and symbol of the True Guide. Rukn is the Black Stone set in the wall of the Ka'bih, the cube-shaped building at Mecca which is the chief object of pilgrimage of the Muslim world. The Maqám or Station of Abraham is near the Ka'bih. Cf. Qur'án 2:119: "Take ye the station of Abraham for a place of prayer"; and again 3:90-91: "The first Temple that was founded for mankind, was that in Becca (i.e., Mecca) . . . In it are evident signs, even the standing-place of Abraham: and he who entereth it is safe." These last four references will be found on pages 164, 179, and 181 of this text.

The foregoing is admittedly minimal in the way of a gloss, since this book is allusively very rich and offers abundant material for study.

5.

The *Epistle to the Son of the Wolf* is still another proof, if more proof were needed, that the Prophet Figure has arisen again, as He did in the past. That the mystery which surrounds us has spoken again, through the mouth of a human being. That the old pattern—of Herald, Prophet, martyrs, and establishment of the Faith—has been repeated in our times. That the promises of previous Faiths as to the advent of the Day of God have at last been redeemed. In that Tablet to the Sháh of Persia, whose bearer was put to death, Bahá'u'lláh, the Glory of God, sums up His case:

"This thing is not from Me, but from One Who is Almighty and All-Knowing. And He bade Me lift up My voice between earth and heaven, and for this there befell Me what hath caused the tears of every man of understanding to flow. The learning current amongst men I studied not; their schools I entered not. Ask of the city wherein I dwelt, that thou mayest be well assured that I am not of them who speak falsely. This is but a leaf which the winds of the will of thy Lord, the Almighty, the All-Praised, have stirred. Can it be still when the tempestuous winds are blowing?

Marzieh Gail
1953

Editorial Note: Before his passing in 1957, Shoghi Effendi appointed twenty-seven Hands of the Cause of God charged with the propagation and protection of the Faith. Through their efforts the election of the first Universal House of Justice was called in April 1963. At that time this supreme administrative institution of the Bahá'í Faith was elected by the fifty-six existing national administrative bodies, in accordance with provisions of the Writings of Bahá'u'lláh. Through a series of global teaching plans, begun in 1953, the Faith has spread to 168 independent countries and 50 overseas departments. [1991]

EPISTLE TO THE SON OF THE WOLF

Praise be to God, the Eternal that perisheth not, the Everlasting that declineth not, the Self-Subsisting that altereth not. He it is Who is transcendent in His sovereignty, Who is manifest through His signs, and is hidden through His mysteries. He it is at Whose bidding the standard of the Most Exalted Word hath been lifted up in the world of creation, and the banner of "He doeth whatsoever He willeth" raised amidst all peoples. He it is Who hath revealed His Cause for the guidance of His creatures, and sent down His verses to demonstrate His Proof and His Testimony, and embellished the preface of the Book of Man with the ornament of utterance through His saying: "The God of Mercy hath taught the Qur'án, hath created man, and taught him articulate speech." No God is there but Him, the One, the Peerless, the Powerful, the Mighty, the Beneficent.

The light that is shed from the heaven of bounty, and the benediction that shineth from the dawning-place of the will of God, the Lord of the Kingdom of Names, rest upon Him Who is the Supreme Mediator, the Most Exalted Pen, Him Whom God hath made the dawning-place of His most excellent names and the dayspring of His most exalted attributes. Through Him the light of unity hath shone forth above the horizon of the world, and the law of oneness hath been revealed amidst the nations, who, with radiant faces, have turned towards the Supreme Horizon, and acknowledged that which the Tongue of Utterance hath spoken in the kingdom of His knowledge: "Earth and heaven, glory and dominion, are God's, the Omnipotent, the Almighty, the Lord of grace abounding!"

Give ear, O distinguished divine, unto the voice of this Wronged One. He verily, counselleth thee for the sake of God, and exhorteth thee unto that which will cause thee to draw nigh unto Him under all conditions. He, in truth, is the All-Possessing, the Exalted. Know thou that the ear of man hath been created that it may hearken unto the Divine Voice on this Day that hath been mentioned in all the Books, Scriptures, and Tablets. Purify thou, first, thy soul with the waters of renunciation, and adorn thine head with the crown of the fear of God, and thy temple with the ornament of reliance upon Him. Arise, then, and, with thy face set towards the Most Great House, the Spot round which, as decreed by the Eternal King, all that dwell on earth must circle, recite:

[2]

"O God, my God, and my Desire, and my Adored One, and my Master, and my Mainstay, and my utmost Hope, and my supreme Aspiration! Thou seest me turning towards Thee, holding fast unto the cord of Thy bounty, clinging to the hem of Thy generosity, acknowledging the sanctity of Thy Self and the purity of Thine Essence, and testifying to Thy unity and Thy oneness. I bear witness that Thou art the One, the Single, the Incomparable, the Ever-Abiding. Thou didst not take unto Thyself a partner in Thy dominion, nor didst Thou choose a peer for Thyself upon earth. All created things have borne witness unto that which the Tongue of Thy grandeur hath testified ere their creation. Verily Thou art God; there is none other God but Thee! From everlasting Thou wast sanctified from the mention of Thy servants, and exalted above the description of Thy creatures. Thou beholdest, O Lord, the ignorant seeking the ocean of Thy knowledge, the sore athirst the living waters of Thine utterance, the abased the tabernacle of Thy glory, the poor the treasury of Thy riches, the suppliant the dawning-place of Thy wisdom, the weak the source of Thy strength, the wretched the heaven of Thy bounty, the dumb the kingdom of Thy mention.

"I testify, O my God, and my King, that Thou hast created me to remember Thee, to glorify Thee, and to aid Thy Cause. And yet, I have aided Thine enemies, who have broken Thy Covenant, who have cast away Thy Book, disbelieved in Thee, and repudiated Thy signs. Alas, alas, for my waywardness, and my shame, and my sinfulness, and my wrong-doing that have withheld me from the depths of the ocean of Thy unity and from fathoming the sea of Thy mercy. Wherefore, alas, alas! and again alas, alas! for my wretchedness and the grievousness of my transgressions! Thou didst call me into being, O my God, to exalt Thy Word, and to manifest Thy Cause. My heedlessness, however, hath deterred me and compassed me about, in such wise that I have arisen to blot out Thy signs, and to shed the blood of Thy loved ones, and of the dawning-places of Thy signs, and of the daysprings of Thy revelation, and of the repositories of Thy mysteries.

"O Lord, my Lord! and again, O Lord, my Lord! and yet again, O Lord, my Lord! I bear witness that by reason of mine iniquity the fruits of the tree of Thy justice have fallen, and through the fire of my rebelliousness the hearts of such of Thy creatures as enjoy near access to Thee were consumed, and the souls of the sincere among Thy servants have melted. O wretched, wretched that I am! O the cruelties, the glaring cruelties, I inflicted! Woe is me, woe is me, for my remoteness from Thee, and for my waywardness, and mine ignorance, and my baseness, and my repudiation of Thee, and my protests against Thee! How many the days during which Thou didst bid Thy servants and Thy loved ones to protect me, whilst I commanded them to harm Thee and to harm them that Thou didst trust! And how numerous the nights during which Thou didst graciously remember me, and didst show me Thy path, whilst I turned away from Thee and from Thy signs! By Thy glory! O Thou Who art the Hope of such as have acknowledged Thy unity, and the Desire of the hearts of them that are rid of all attachment to any save Thee! I find no succorer except Thee, nor king, nor refuge, nor haven besides Thyself. Alas, alas! My turning away from Thee hath burnt up the veil of mine integrity, and my denial of Thee hath rent asunder the covering cast over mine honor. O would that I were beneath the depths of the earth, so that my evil deeds would remain unknown to Thy servants! Thou seest the sinner, O my Lord, who hath turned towards the dawning-place of Thy forgiveness and Thy bounty, and the mountain of iniquity that hath sought the heaven of Thy mercy and pardon. Alas, alas! My mighty sins have prevented me from approaching the court of Thy mercy, and my monstrous deeds have caused me to stray far from the sanctuary of Thy presence. Indeed, I am he that hath failed in duty towards Thee, and hath broken Thy Covenant and Thy Testament, and committed that which hath made the dwellers of the cities of Thy justice, and the dawning-places of Thy grace in Thy realms, to lament. I testify, O my God, that I have put away Thy commandments, and clung to the dictates of my passions, and have cast away the statutes of Thy Book, and seized the book of mine own desire. O misery, misery! As mine iniquities waxed greater and greater, Thy forbearance towards me augmented, and as the fire of my rebelliousness grew fiercer, the more did Thy forgiveness and Thy grace seek to smother up its flame. By the power of Thy might! O Thou Who art the desire of the world· and the Best-Beloved of the nations! Thy long-suffering hath puffed me up, and Thy patience hath emboldened me. Thou beholdest, O my God, the tears that my shame hath caused to flow, and the sighs which my heedlessness hath led me to utter. I swear by the greatness of Thy majesty! I can find for myself no habitation save beneath the shadow of the court of Thy bounty, nor any refuge except under the canopy of Thy mercy. Thou seest me in the midst of a sea of despair and of hopelessness, after Thou didst cause me to hear Thy words "Despair not." By Thy power! My sore injustice hath severed the cord of my hope, and my rebellion hath darkened my face before the throne of Thy justice. Thou beholdest, O my God, him who is as one dead fallen at the door of Thy favor, ashamed to seek from the hand of Thy loving-kindness the living waters of Thy pardon. Thou hast given me a tongue wherewith to remember and praise Thee, and yet it uttereth that which hath caused the souls of such of Thy chosen ones as are nigh unto Thee to melt, and the hearts of the sincere amongst the dwellers of the habitations of holiness to be consumed. Thou hast given me eyes to witness Thy signs, and to behold Thy verses, and to contemplate the revelations of Thine handiwork, but I have rejected Thy will, and have committed what hath caused the faithful among Thy creatures and the detached amidst Thy servants to groan. Thou hast given me ears that I may incline them unto Thy praise and Thy celebration, and unto that which Thou didst send down from the heaven of Thy bounty and the firmament of Thy will. And yet, alas, alas, I have forsaken Thy Cause, and have commanded Thy servants to blaspheme against Thy trusted ones and Thy loved ones, and have acted, before the throne of Thy justice, in such wise that those that have recognized Thy unity and are wholly devoted to Thee among the dwellers of Thy realm mourned with a sore lamentation. I know not, O my God, which among my evil doings to mention before the billowing ocean of Thy favor, nor which of my trespasses to declare when face to face with the splendors of the suns of Thy goodly gifts and bounties.

"I beseech Thee, this very moment, by the mysteries of Thy Book, and by the things hid in Thy knowledge, and by the pearls that lie concealed within the shells of the ocean of Thy mercy, to reckon me among such as Thou didst mention in Thy Book and describe in Thy Tablets. Hast Thou decreed for me, O my God, any joy after this tribulation, or any relief to

[7]

succeed this affliction, or any ease to follow this trouble? Alas, alas! Thou hast ordained that every pulpit be set apart for Thy mention, and for the glorification of Thy Word, and the revelation of Thy Cause, but I have ascended it to proclaim the violation of Thy Covenant, and have spoken unto Thy servants such words as have caused the dwellers of the Tabernacles of Thy majesty and the denizens of the Cities of Thy wisdom to lament. How often hast Thou sent down the food of Thine utterance out of the heaven of Thy bounty, and I denied it; and how numerous the occasions on which Thou hast summoned me to the soft flowing waters of Thy mercy, and I have chosen to turn away therefrom, by reason of my having followed my own wish and desire! By Thy glory! I know not for which sin to beg Thy forgiveness and implore Thy pardon, nor from which of mine iniquities to turn aside unto the Court of Thy bounteousness and the Sanctuary of Thy favor. Such are my sins and trespasses that no man can number them, nor pen describe them. I implore Thee, O Thou that turnest darkness into light, and revealest Thy mysteries on the Sinai of Thy Revelation, to aid me, at all times, to put my trust in Thee, and to commit mine affairs unto Thy care. Make me, then, O my God, content with that which the finger of Thy decree hath traced, and the pen of Thy ordinance hath written. Potent art Thou to do what pleaseth Thee, and in Thy grasp are the reins of all that are in heaven and on earth. No God is there but Thee, the All-knowing, the All-Wise."

O Shaykh! Know thou that neither the calumnies which men may utter, nor their denials, nor any cavils they may raise, can harm him that hath clung to the cord of the grace, and seized the hem of the mercy, of the Lord of creation. By God! He, the Glory of God (Bahá), hath spoken not from mere impulse. He that hath given Him a voice is He that hath given a voice unto all things, that they may praise and glorify Him. There is none other God but Him, the One, the Incomparable, the Lord of strength, the Unconditioned.

They whose sight is keen, whose ears are retentive, whose hearts are enlightened, and whose breasts are dilated, recognize both truth and falsehood, and distinguish the one from the other. Recite thou this prayer that hath flowed from the tongue of this Wronged One, and ponder thereon with a heart rid of all attachment, and with ears that are pure and sanctified, be attentive to its meaning, that haply thou mayest inhale the breath of detachment and have pity upon thyself and upon others:

"My God, the Object of my adoration, the Goal of my desire, the All-Bountiful, the Most Compassionate! All life is of Thee, and all power lieth within the grasp of Thine omnipotence. Whosoever Thou exaltest is raised above the angels, and attaineth the station: 'Verily, We uplifted him to a place on high!'; and whosoever Thou dost abase is made lower than dust, nay, less than nothing. O Divine Providence! Though wicked, sinful, and intemperate, we still seek from Thee a 'seat of truth,' and long to behold the countenance of the Omnipotent King. It is Thine to command, and all sovereignty belongeth to Thee, and the realm of might boweth before Thy behest. Everything Thou doest is pure justice, nay, the very essence of grace. One gleam from the splendors of Thy Name, the All-Merciful, sufficeth to banish and blot out every trace of sinfulness from the world, and a single breath from the breezes of the Day of Thy Revelation is enough to adorn all mankind with a fresh attire. Vouchsafe Thy strength, O Almighty One, unto Thy weak creatures, and quicken them who are as dead, that haply they may find Thee, and may be led unto the ocean of Thy guidance, and may remain steadfast in Thy Cause. Should the fragrance of Thy praise be shed abroad by any of the divers tongues of the world, out of the East or out of the West, it would, verily, be prized and greatly cherished. If such tongues, however, be deprived of that fragrance, they assuredly would be unworthy of any mention, in word or yet in thought. We beg of Thee, O Providence, to show Thy way unto all men, and to guide them aright. Thou art, verily, the Almighty, the Most Powerful, the All-Knowing, the All-Seeing."

We beseech God to aid thee to be just and fair-minded, and to acquaint thee with the things that were hidden from the eyes of men. He, in truth, is the Mighty, the Unconstrained. We ask thee to reflect upon that which hath been revealed, and to be fair and just in thy speech, that perchance the splendors of the day-star of truthfulness and sincerity may shine forth, and may deliver thee from the darkness of ignorance, and illumine the world with the light of knowledge. This Wronged One hath frequented no school, neither hath He attended the controversies of the learned. By My life! Not of Mine own volition have I revealed Myself, but God, of His own choosing, hath manifested Me. In the Tablet, addressed to His Majesty the S͟háh—may God, blessed and glorified be He, assist him—these words have streamed from the tongue of this Wronged One:

"O King! I was but a man like others, asleep upon My couch, when lo, the breezes of the All-Glorious were wafted over Me, and taught Me the knowledge of all that hath been. This thing is not from Me, but from One Who is Almighty and All-Knowing. And He bade Me lift up My voice between earth and heaven, and for this there befell Me what hath caused the tears of every man of understanding to flow. The learning current amongst men I studied not; their schools I entered not. Ask of the city wherein I dwelt, that thou mayest be well assured that I am not of them who speak falsely. This is but a leaf which the winds of the will of thy Lord, the Almighty, the All-Praised, have stirred. Can it be still when the tempestuous winds are blowing? Nay, by Him Who is the Lord of all Names and Attributes! They move it as they list. The evanescent is as nothing before Him Who is the Ever-Abiding. His all-compelling summons hath reached Me, and caused Me to speak His praise amidst all people. I was indeed as one dead when His behest was uttered. The hand of the will of thy Lord, the Compassionate, the Merciful, transformed Me."

Now is the moment in which to cleanse thyself with the waters of detachment that have flowed out from the Supreme Pen, and to ponder, wholly for the sake of God, those things which, time and again, have been sent down or manifested, and then to strive, as much as lieth in thee, to quench, through the power of wisdom and the force of thy utterance, the fire of enmity and hatred which smouldereth in the hearts of the peoples of the world. The Divine Messengers have been sent down, and their Books were revealed, for the purpose of promoting the knowledge of God, and of furthering unity and fellowship amongst men. But now behold, how they have made the Law of God a cause and pretext for perversity and hatred. How pitiful, how regrettable, that most men are cleaving fast to, and have busied themselves with, the things they possess, and are unaware of, and shut out as by a veil from, the things God possesseth!

Say: "O God, my God! Attire mine head with the

crown of justice, and my temple with the ornament of equity. Thou, verily, art the Possessor of all gifts and bounties."

Justice and equity are twin Guardians that watch over men. From them are revealed such blessed and perspicuous words as are the cause of the well-being of the world and the protection of the nations.

These words have streamed from the pen of this Wronged One in one of His Tablets: "The purpose of the one true God, exalted be His glory, hath been to bring forth the Mystic Gems out of the mine of man—they Who are the Dawning-Places of His Cause and the Repositories of the pearls of His knowledge; for, God Himself, glorified be He, is the Unseen, the One concealed and hidden from the eyes of men. Consider what the Merciful hath revealed in the Qur'án: No vision taketh in Him, but He taketh in all vision, and He is the Subtile, the All-Informed!"

That the divers communions of the earth, and the manifold systems of religious belief, should never be allowed to foster the feelings of animosity among men, is, in this Day, of the essence of the Faith of God and His Religion. These principles and laws, these firmly-established and mighty systems, have proceeded from one Source, and are rays of one Light. That they differ one from another is to be attributed to the varying requirements of the ages in which they were promulgated.

Gird up the loins of your endeavor, O people of

Bahá, that haply the tumult of religious dissension and strife that agitateth the peoples of the earth may be stilled, that every trace of it may be completely obliterated. For the love of God, and them that serve Him, arise to aid this sublime and momentous Revelation. Religious fanaticism and hatred are a world-devouring fire, whose violence none can quench. The Hand of Divine power can, alone, deliver mankind from this desolating affliction. Consider the war that hath involved the two Nations, how both sides have renounced their possessions and their lives. How many the villages that were completely wiped out!

The utterance of God is a lamp, whose light are these words: Ye are the fruits of one tree, and the leaves of one branch. Deal ye one with another with the utmost love and harmony, with friendliness and fellowship. He Who is the Day-Star of Truth beareth Me witness! So powerful is the light of unity that it can illuminate the whole earth. The One true God, He Who knoweth all things, Himself testifieth to the truth of these words.

Exert yourselves that ye may attain this transcendent and most sublime station, the station that can insure the protection and security of all mankind. This goal excelleth every other goal, and this aspiration is the monarch of all aspirations. So long, however, as the thick clouds of oppression, which obscure the day-star of justice, remain undispelled, it would be difficult for the glory of this station to be unveiled to men's eyes. These thick clouds are the exponents of idle fancies and vain imaginings, who are none other but the divines of Persia. At one time We spoke in the language of the lawgiver; at another in that of the truth-seeker and the mystic, and yet Our supreme purpose and highest wish hath always been to disclose the glory and sublimity of this station. God, verily, is a sufficient witness!

Consort with all men, O people of Bahá, in a spirit of friendliness and fellowship. If ye be aware of a certain truth, if ye possess a jewel, of which others are deprived, share it with them in a language of utmost kindliness and good-will. If it be accepted, if it fulfill its purpose, your object is attained. If anyone should refuse it, leave him unto himself, and beseech God to guide him. Beware lest ye deal unkindly with him. A kindly tongue is the lodestone of the hearts of men. It is the bread of the spirit, it clotheth the words with meaning, it is the fountain of the light of wisdom and understanding.

By "divines" in the passage cited above is meant those men who outwardly attire themselves with the raiment of knowledge, but who inwardly are deprived therefrom. In this connection, We quote from the Tablet addressed to His Majesty the Sháh, certain passages from the "Hidden Words" which were revealed by the Abhá Pen under the name of the "Book of Fáṭimih," the blessings of God be upon her!

"O ye that are foolish, yet have a name to be wise! Wherefore do ye wear the guise of the shepherd, when inwardly ye have become wolves, intent upon My flock? Ye are even as the star, which riseth ere the dawn, and which, though it seem radiant and luminous, leadeth the wayfarers of My city astray into the paths of perdition."

And likewise He saith: "O ye seeming fair yet inwardly foul! Ye are like clear but bitter water, which to outward seeming is crystal pure but of which, when tested by the Divine Assayer, not a drop is accepted. Yea, the sunbeam falls alike upon the dust and the mirror, yet differ they in reflection even as doth the star from the earth: nay, immeasurable is the difference!"

And also He saith: "O essence of desire! At many a dawn have I turned from the realms of the Placeless unto thine abode, and found thee on the bed of ease busied with others than Myself. Thereupon, even as the flash of the spirit, I returned to the realms of celestial glory, and breathed it not in My retreats above unto the hosts of holiness."

And again He saith: "O bond slave of the world! Many a dawn hath the breeze of My loving-kindness wafted over thee and found thee upon the bed of heedlessness fast asleep. Bewailing then thy plight it returned whence it came."

Those divines, however, who are truly adorned with the ornament of knowledge and of a goodly character are, verily, as a head to the body of the world, and as eyes to the nations. The guidance of men hath, at all times, been, and is, dependent upon such blessed souls. We beseech God to graciously aid them to do His will and pleasure. He, in truth, is the Lord of all men, the Lord of this world and of the next.

O Shaykh! We have learned that thou hast turned away from Us, and protested against Us, in such wise that thou hast bidden the people to curse Me, and decreed that the blood of the servants of God be shed. God requite him who said: "Willingly will I obey the judge who hath so strangely decreed that my blood be spilt at Hill and at Ḥaram!" Verily I say: Whatever befalleth in the path of God is the beloved of the soul and the desire of the heart. Deadly poison in His path is pure honey, and every tribulation a draught of crystal water. In the Tablet to His Majesty the Sháh it is written: "By Him Who is the Truth! I fear no tribulation in His path, nor any affliction in My love for Him. Verily God hath made adversity as a morning dew upon His green pasture, and a wick for His lamp which lighteth earth and heaven."

Set thine heart towards Him Who is the Kaaba of God, the Help in Peril, the Self-Subsisting, and raise thou thine hands with such firm conviction as shall cause the hands of all created things to be lifted up towards the heaven of the grace of God, the Lord of all worlds. Turn, then, thy face towards Him in such wise that the faces of all beings will turn in the direction of His shining and luminous Horizon, and say: "Thou seest me, O my Lord, with my face turned towards the heaven of Thy bounty and the ocean of Thy favor, withdrawn from all else beside Thee. I ask of Thee, by the splendors of the Sun of Thy revelation on Sinai, and the effulgences of the Orb of Thy grace which shineth from the horizon of Thy Name, the Ever-Forgiving, to grant me Thy pardon and to have mercy upon me. Write down, then, for me with Thy pen of glory that which will exalt me through Thy Name in the world of creation. Aid me, O my Lord, to set myself towards Thee, and to hearken unto the voice of Thy loved ones, whom the powers of the earth have failed to weaken, and the dominion of the nations has been powerless to withhold from Thee, and who, advancing towards Thee, have said: 'God is our Lord, the Lord of all who are in heaven and all who are on earth!' "

O Shaykh! Verily I say, the seal of the Choice Wine hath, in the name of Him Who is the Self-Subsisting, been broken; withhold not thyself therefrom. This Wronged One speaketh wholly for the sake of God; thou too shouldst, likewise, for the sake of God, meditate upon those things that have been sent down and manifested, that haply thou mayest, on this blessed Day, take thy portion of the liberal effusions of Him Who is truly the All-Bountiful, and mayest not remain deprived thereof. This indeed would not be hard for God. Dust-made Adam was raised up, through the Word of God, to the heavenly throne, and a mere fisherman was made the repository of Divine wisdom, and Abú-Dhar, the shepherd, became a prince of the nations!

This Day, O Shaykh, hath never been, nor is it now, the Day whereon man-made arts and sciences can be regarded as a true standard for men, since it hath been recognized that He Who was wholly unversed in any of them hath ascended the throne of purest gold, and occupied the seat of honor in the council of knowledge, whilst the acknowledged exponent and repository of these arts and sciences remained utterly deprived. By "arts and sciences" is meant those which begin with words and end with words. Such arts and sciences, however, as are productive of good results, and bring forth their fruit, and are conducive to the well-being and tranquility of men have been, and will remain, acceptable before God. Wert thou to give ear to My voice, thou wouldst cast away all thy possessions, and wouldst set thy face towards the Spot wherein the ocean of wisdom and of utterance hath surged, and the sweet savors of the loving-kindness of thy Lord, the Compassionate, have wafted.

We deem it advisable, in this connection, to recount briefly some past events, that perchance they may be the means of vindicating the cause of equity and justice. At the time when His Majesty the Sháh, may God, his Lord, the Most Merciful, aid him through His strengthening grace, was planning a journey to Iṣfahán, this Wronged One, having obtained his permission, visited the holy and luminous resting-places of the Imáms, may the blessings of God be upon them! Upon Our return, We proceeded to Lavásán on account of the excessive heat prevailing in the capital. Following Our departure, there occurred the attempt upon the life of His Majesty, may God, exalted and glorified be He, assist him. Those days were troublous days, and the fires of hatred burned high. Many were arrested, among them this Wronged One. By the righteousness of God! We were in no wise connected with that evil deed, and Our innocence was indisputably established by the tribunals. Nevertheless, they apprehended Us, and from Níyávarán, which was then the residence of His Majesty, conducted Us, on foot and in chains, with bared head and bare feet, to the dungeon of Ṭihrán. A brutal man, accompanying Us on horseback, snatched off Our hat, whilst We were being hurried along by a troop of executioners and officials. We were consigned for four months to a place foul beyond comparison. As to the dungeon in which this Wronged One and others similarly wronged were confined, a dark and narrow pit were preferable. Upon Our arrival We were first conducted along a pitch-black corridor, from whence We descended three steep flights of stairs to the place of confinement assigned to Us. The dungeon was wrapped in thick darkness, and Our fellow-prisoners numbered nearly a hundred and fifty souls: thieves, assassins and highwaymen. Though crowded, it had no other outlet than the passage by which We entered. No pen can depict that place, nor any tongue describe its loathsome smell. Most of these men had neither clothes nor bedding to lie on. God alone knoweth what befell Us in that most foul-smelling and gloomy place!

Day and night, while confined in that dungeon, We meditated upon the deeds, the condition, and the conduct of the Bábís, wondering what could have led a people so high-minded, so noble, and of such intelligence, to perpetrate such an audacious and outrageous act against the person of His Majesty. This Wronged One, thereupon, decided to arise, after His release from prison, and undertake, with the utmost vigor, the task of regenerating this people.

One night, in a dream, these exalted words were heard on every side: "Verily, We shall render Thee victorious by Thyself and by Thy Pen. Grieve Thou not for that which hath befallen Thee, neither be Thou afraid, for Thou art in safety. Erelong will God raise up the treasures of the earth—men who will aid Thee through Thyself and through Thy Name, wherewith God hath revived the hearts of such as have recognized Him."

And when this Wronged One went forth out of

His prison, We journeyed, in pursuance of the order of His Majesty the Sháh—may God, exalted be He, protect him—to 'Iráq, escorted by officers in the service of the esteemed and honored governments of Persia and Russia. After Our arrival, We revealed, as a copious rain, by the aid of God and His Divine Grace and mercy, Our verses, and sent them to various parts of the world. We exhorted all men, and particularly this people, through Our wise counsels and loving admonitions, and forbade them to engage in sedition, quarrels, disputes and conflict. As a result of this, and by the grace of God, waywardness and folly were changed into piety and understanding, and weapons converted into instruments of peace.

During the days I lay in the prison of Ṭihrán, though the galling weight of the chains and the stench-filled air allowed Me but little sleep, still in those infrequent moments of slumber I felt as if something flowed from the crown of My head over My breast, even as a mighty torrent that precipitateth itself upon the earth from the summit of a lofty mountain. Every limb of My body would, as a result, be set afire. At such moments My tongue recited what no man could bear to hear.

We shall herewith cite a few passages from Tablets specifically revealed to this people, so that every one may know of a certainty that this Wronged One hath acted in a manner which hath been pleasing and

[22]

acceptable unto men endued with insight, and unto such as are the exponents of justice and equity:

"O ye friends of God in His cities and His loved ones in His lands! This Wronged One enjoineth on you honesty and piety. Blessed the city that shineth by their light. Through them man is exalted, and the door of security is unlocked before the face of all creation. Happy the man that cleaveth fast unto them, and recognizeth their virtue, and woe betide him that denieth their station."

And in another connection these words were revealed: "We enjoin the servants of God and His handmaidens to be pure and to fear God, that they may shake off the slumber of their corrupt desires, and turn toward God, the Maker of the heavens and of the earth. Thus have We commanded the faithful when the Day-Star of the world shone forth from the horizon of 'Iráq. My imprisonment doeth Me no harm, neither the tribulations I suffer, nor the things that have befallen Me at the hands of My oppressors. That which harmeth Me is the conduct of those who, though they bear My name, yet commit that which maketh My heart and My pen to lament. They that spread disorder in the land, and lay hands on the property of others, and enter a house without leave of its owner, We, verily, are clear of them, unless they repent and return unto God, the Ever-Forgiving, the Most Merciful."

[23]

And in another connection: "O peoples of the earth! Haste ye to do the pleasure of God, and war ye valiantly, as it behooveth you to war, for the sake of proclaiming His resistless and immovable Cause. We have decreed that war shall be waged in the path of God with the armies of wisdom and utterance, and of a goodly character and praiseworthy deeds. Thus hath it been decided by Him Who is the All-Powerful, the Almighty. There is no glory for him that committeth disorder on the earth after it hath been made so good. Fear God, O people, and be not of them that act unjustly."

And again in another connection: "Revile ye not one another. We, verily, have come to unite and weld together all that dwell on earth. Unto this beareth witness what the ocean of Mine utterance hath revealed amongst men, and yet most of the people have gone astray. If anyone revile you, or trouble touch you, in the path of God, be patient, and put your trust in Him Who heareth, Who seeth. He, in truth, witnesseth, and perceiveth, and doeth what He pleaseth, through the power of His sovereignty. He, verily, is the Lord of strength, and of might. In the Book of God, the Mighty, the Great, ye have been forbidden to engage in contention and conflict. Lay fast hold on whatever will profit you, and profit the peoples of the world. Thus commandeth you the King of Eternity, Who is manifest in His Most Great Name. He, verily, is the Ordainer, the All-Wise."

And yet again in another connection: "Beware lest ye shed the blood of any one. Unsheathe the sword of your tongue from the scabbard of utterance, for therewith ye can conquer the citadels of men's hearts. We have abolished the law to wage holy war against each other. God's mercy hath, verily, encompassed all created things, if ye do but understand."

And yet again in another connection: "O people! Spread not disorder in the land, and shed not the blood of any one, and consume not the substance of others wrongfully, neither follow every accursed prattler."

And still again in another connection: "The Sun of Divine Utterance can never set, neither can its radiance be extinguished. These sublime words have, in this day, been heard from the Lote-Tree beyond which there is no passing: 'I belong to him that loveth Me, that holdeth fast My commandments, and casteth away the things forbidden him in My Book.'"

And still again in another connection: "This is the day to make mention of God, to celebrate His praise, and to serve Him; deprive not yourselves thereof. Ye are the letters of the words, and the words of the Book. Ye are the saplings which the hand of Loving-kindness hath planted in the soil of mercy, and which the showers of bounty have made to flourish. He hath protected you from the mighty winds of misbelief, and the tempestuous gales of impiety, and nurtured you with the hands of His loving providence. Now is the time for you to put forth your leaves, and yield your fruit. The fruits of the tree of man have ever been and are goodly deeds and a praiseworthy character. Withhold not these fruits from the heedless. If they be accepted, your end is attained, and the purpose of life achieved. If not, leave them in their pastime of vain disputes. Strive, O people of God, that haply the hearts of the divers kindreds of the earth may, through the waters of your forbearance and loving-kindness, be cleansed and sanctified from animosity and hatred, and be made worthy and befitting recipients of the splendors of the Sun of Truth."

In the fourth Ishráq (splendor) of the Ishráqát (Tablet of Splendors) We have mentioned: "Every cause needeth a helper. In this Revelation the hosts which can render it victorious are the hosts of praiseworthy deeds and upright character. The leader and commander of these hosts hath ever been the fear of God, a fear that encompasseth all things, and reigneth over all things."

In the third Tajallí (effulgence) of the Book of Tajallíyát (Book of Effulgences) We have mentioned: "Arts, crafts and sciences uplift the world of being, and are conducive to its exaltation. Knowledge is as wings to man's life, and a ladder for his ascent. Its acquisition is incumbent upon everyone. The knowledge of such sciences, however, should be acquired as can profit the peoples of the earth, and not those which begin with words and end with words.

Great indeed is the claim of scientists and craftsmen on the peoples of the world. Unto this beareth witness the Mother Book in this conspicuous station."

In truth, knowledge is a veritable treasure for man, and a source of glory, of bounty, of joy, of exaltation, of cheer and gladness unto him. Happy the man that cleaveth unto it, and woe betide the heedless.

It is incumbent upon thee to summon the people, under all conditions, to whatever will cause them to show forth spiritual characteristics and goodly deeds, so that all may become aware of that which is the cause of human upliftment, and may, with the utmost endeavor, direct themselves towards the most sublime Station and the Pinnacle of Glory. The fear of God hath ever been the prime factor in the education of His creatures. Well is it with them that have attained thereunto!

The first word which the Abhá Pen hath revealed and inscribed on the first leaf of Paradise is this: "Verily I say: The fear of God hath ever been a sure defence and a safe stronghold for all the peoples of the world. It is the chief cause of the protection of mankind, and the supreme instrument for its preservation. Indeed, there existeth in man a faculty which deterreth him from, and guardeth him against, whatever is unworthy and unseemly, and which is known as his sense of shame. This, however, is confined to but a few; all have not possessed, and do not possess, it. It is incumbent upon the kings and the spiritual leaders of the world to lay fast hold on religion, inasmuch as through it the fear of God is instilled in all else but Him."

The second word We have recorded on the second leaf of Paradise is the following: "The Pen of the Divine Expounder exhorteth, at this moment, the manifestations of authority and the sources of power, namely the kings and rulers of the earth—may God assist them—and enjoineth them to uphold the cause of religion, and to cleave unto it. Religion is, verily, the chief instrument for the establishment of order in the world, and of tranquillity amongst its peoples. The weakening of the pillars of religion hath strengthened the foolish, and emboldened them, and made them more arrogant. Verily I say: The greater the decline of religion, the more grievous the waywardness of the ungodly. This cannot but lead in the end to chaos and confusion. Hear Me, O men of insight, and be warned, ye who are endued with discernment!"

It is Our hope that thou wilt hear with attentive ears the things We have mentioned unto thee, that perchance thou mayest turn men away from the things they possess to the things that God possesseth. We entreat God to deliver the light of equity and the sun of justice from the thick clouds of waywardness, and cause them to shine forth upon men. No light can compare with the light of justice. The establish-

ment of order in the world and the tranquillity of
the nations depend upon it.

In the Book of Utterance these exalted words have
been written down and recorded: "Say, O friends!
Strive that haply the tribulations suffered by this
Wronged One and by you, in the path of God, may
not prove to have been in vain. Cling ye to the hem
of virtue, and hold fast to the cord of trustworthiness and piety. Concern yourselves with the things
that benefit mankind, and not with your corrupt and
selfish desires. O ye followers of this Wronged One!
Ye are the shepherds of mankind; liberate ye your
flocks from the wolves of evil passions and desires,
and adorn them with the ornament of the fear of
God. This is the firm commandment which hath, at
this moment, flowed out from the Pen of Him Who
is the Ancient of Days. By the righteousness of God!
The sword of a virtuous character and upright conduct is sharper than blades of steel. The voice of the
true Faith calleth aloud, at this moment, and saith:
O people! Verily, the Day is come, and My Lord
hath made Me to shine forth with a light whose
splendor hath eclipsed the suns of utterance. Fear ye
the Merciful, and be not of them that have gone
astray."

The third word we have recorded on the third leaf
of Paradise is this: "O son of man! If thine eyes be
turned towards mercy, forsake the things that profit

thee, and cleave unto that which will profit mankind. And if thine eyes be turned towards justice, choose thou for thy neighbor that which thou choosest for thyself. Humility exalteth man to the heaven of glory and power, whilst pride abaseth him to the depths of wretchedness and degradation. Great is the Day, and mighty the Call! In one of Our Tablets We have revealed these exalted words: 'Were the world of the spirit to be wholly converted into the sense of hearing, it could then claim to be worthy to hearken unto the Voice that calleth from the Supreme Horizon; for otherwise, these ears that are defiled with lying tales have never been, nor are they now, fit to hear it.' Well is it with them that hearken; and woe betide the wayward."

We pray God—exalted be His glory—and cherish the hope that He may graciously assist the manifestations of affluence and power and the dayspring of sovereignty and glory, the kings of the earth—may God aid them through His strengthening grace—to establish the Lesser Peace. This, indeed, is the greatest means for insuring the tranquillity of the nations. It is incumbent upon the Sovereigns of the world— may God assist them—unitedly to hold fast unto this Peace, which is the chief instrument for the protection of all mankind. It is Our hope that they will arise to achieve what will be conducive to the well-being of man. It is their duty to convene an all-inclusive assembly, which either they themselves or

their ministers will attend, and to enforce whatever
measures are required to establish unity and concord
amongst men. They must put away the weapons of
war, and turn to the instruments of universal reconstruction. Should one king rise up against another,
all the other kings must arise to deter him. Arms and
armaments will, then, be no more needed beyond
that which is necessary to insure the internal security
of their respective countries. If they attain unto this
all-surpassing blessing, the people of each nation will
pursue, with tranquillity and contentment, their own
occupations, and the groanings and lamentations of
most men would be silenced. We beseech God to aid
them to do His will and pleasure. He, verily, is the
Lord of the throne on high and of earth below, and
the Lord of this world and of the world to come. It
would be preferable and more fitting that the highly-
honored kings themselves should attend such an assembly, and proclaim their edicts. Any king who will
arise and carry out this task, he, verily will, in the
sight of God, become the cynosure of all kings.
Happy is he, and great is his blessedness!

In this land, every time men are conscripted for
the army, a great terror seizeth the people. Every
nation augmenteth, each year, its forces, for their
ministers of war are insatiable in their desire to add
fresh recruits to their battalions. We have learned
that the government of Persia—may God assist them
—have, likewise, decided to reinforce their army. In

the opinion of this Wronged One a force of one hundred thousand fully-equipped and well-disciplined men would suffice. We hope that thou wilt cause the light of justice to shine more brightly. By the righteousness of God! Justice is a powerful force. It is, above all else, the conqueror of the citadels of the hearts and souls of men, and the revealer of the secrets of the world of being, and the standard-bearer of love and bounty.

In the treasuries of the knowledge of God there lieth concealed a knowledge which, when applied, will largely, though not wholly, eliminate fear. This knowledge, however, should be taught from childhood, as it will greatly aid in its elimination. Whatever decreaseth fear increaseth courage. Should the Will of God assist Us, there would flow out from the Pen of the Divine Expounder a lengthy exposition of that which hath been mentioned, and there would be revealed, in the field of arts and sciences, what would renew the world and the nations. A word hath, likewise, been written down and recorded by the Pen of the Most High in the Crimson Book which is capable of fully disclosing that force which is hid in men, nay of redoubling its potency. We implore God—exalted and glorified be He—to graciously assist His servants to do that which is pleasing and acceptable unto Him.

In these days enemies have compassed Us about, and the fire of hatred is kindled. O peoples of the earth! By My life and by your own! This Wronged One hath never had, nor hath He now any desire for leadership. Mine aim hath ever been, and still is, to suppress whatever is the cause of contention amidst the peoples of the earth, and of separation amongst the nations, so that all men may be sanctified from every earthly attachment, and be set free to occupy themselves with their own interests. We entreat Our loved ones not to besmirch the hem of Our raiment with the dust of falsehood, neither to allow references to what they have regarded as miracles and prodigies to debase Our rank and station, or to mar the purity and sanctity of Our name.

Gracious God! This is the day whereon the wise should seek the advice of this Wronged One, and ask Him Who is the Truth what things are conducive to the glory and tranquillity of men. And yet, all are earnestly striving to put out this glorious and shining light, and are diligently seeking either to establish Our guilt, or to voice their protest against Us. Matters have come to such a pass, that the conduct of this Wronged One hath, in every way, been grossly misrepresented, and in a manner which it would be unseemly to mention. One of Our friends hath reported that among the residents of the Great City (Constantinople) he had heard with the greatest regret someone state that, each year, a sum of fifty thousand tumans was being despatched from his native land to 'Akká! It hath not, however, been made

clear who had disbursed the sum, nor through whose
hands it had passed!

Briefly, this Wronged One hath, in the face of all
that hath befallen Him at their hands, and all that
hath been said of Him, endured patiently, and held
His peace, inasmuch as it is Our purpose, through the
loving providence of God—exalted be His glory—
and His surpassing mercy, to abolish, through the
force of Our utterance, all disputes, war, and blood-
shed, from the face of the earth. Under all conditions We have, in spite of what they have said,
endured with seemly patience, and have left them to
God. In answer to this particular imputation, however, We have replied, that if that which he affirmeth
be true, it behooveth him to be thankful to Him Who
is the Lord of all being, and the King of the seen and
unseen, for having raised up in Persia One Who,
though a prisoner and with none to help and assist
Him, hath succeeded in establishing His ascendency
over that land, and in drawing from it a yearly rev-
enue. Such an achievement should be praised rather
than censured, if he be of them that judge equitably.
Should anyone seek to be acquainted with the condition of this Wronged One, let him be told that these
captives whom the world hath persecuted and the nations wronged have, for days and nights, been entirely
denied the barest means of subsistence. We are loth
to mention such things, neither have We had, nor
do We have now, any desire to complain against Our

accuser. Within the walls of this prison a highly-esteemed man was for some time obliged to break stones that he might earn a living, whilst others had, at times, to nourish themselves with that Divine sustenance which is hunger! We entreat God—exalted and glorified be He—to aid all men to be just and fair-minded, and to graciously assist them to repent and return unto Him. He, verily, heareth, and is ready to answer.

Glorified art Thou, O Lord my God! Thou seest what hath befallen this Wronged One at the hands of them that have not associated with Me, and who have arisen to harm and abase Me, in a manner which no pen can describe, nor tongue recount, nor can any Tablet sustain its weight. Thou hearest the cry of Mine heart, and the groaning of Mine inmost being, and the things that have befallen Thy trusted ones in Thy cities and Thy chosen ones in Thy land, at the hands of such as have broken Thy Covenant and Thy Testament. I beseech Thee, O my Lord, by the sighs of Thy lovers throughout the world, and by their lamentation in their remoteness from the court of Thy presence, and by the blood that hath been shed for love of Thee, and by the hearts that have melted in Thy path, to protect Thy loved ones from the cruelty of such as have remained unaware of the mysteries of Thy Name, the Unconstrained. Assist them, O my Lord, by Thy power that hath prevailed over all things, and aid them to be patient and long-suffering. Thou art the All-Powerful, the Almighty, the All-Bountiful. No God is there but Thee, the Generous, the Lord of grace abounding.

In these days there are some who, far from being just and fair-minded, have assaulted Me with the sword of hatred and the spear of enmity, forgetting that it behooveth every fair-minded person to succor Him Whom the world hath cast away and the nations abandoned, and to lay hold on piety and righteousness. Most men have until now failed to discover the purpose of this Wronged One, nor have they known the reason for which He hath been willing to endure countless afflictions. Meanwhile, the voice of Mine heart crieth out these words: "O that My people knew!" This Wronged One, rid of attachment unto all things, uttereth these exalted words: "Waves have encompassed the Ark of God, the Help in Peril, the Self-Subsisting. Fear not the tempestuous gales, O Mariner! He Who causeth the dawn to appear is, verily, with Thee in this darkness that hath struck terror into the hearts of all men, except such as God, the Almighty, the Unconstrained, hath been pleased to spare."

O Shaykh! I swear by the Sun of Truth Which hath risen and shineth above the horizon of this Prison! The betterment of the world hath been the sole aim of this Wronged One. Unto this beareth witness every man of judgment, of discernment, of insight and understanding. Whilst afflicted with trials, He held fast unto the cord of patience and fortitude, and was satisfied with the things which have befallen Him at the hands of His enemies, and was crying out: "I have renounced My desire for Thy desire, O my God, and My will for the revelation of Thy Will. By Thy glory! I desire neither Myself nor My life except for the purpose of serving Thy Cause, and I love not My being save that I may sacrifice it in Thy path. Thou seest and knowest, O my Lord, that those whom We asked to be fair and just, have, unjustly and cruelly, risen up against Us. Openly they were with Me, yet secretly they assisted My foes, who have arisen to dishonor Me. O God, my God! I testify that Thou hast created Thy servants to aid Thy Cause and exalt Thy Word, and yet they have helped Thine enemies. I beseech Thee, by Thy Cause that hath encompassed the world of being, and by Thy Name wherewith Thou hast subjected the seen and unseen, to adorn the peoples of the earth with the light of Thy justice, and to illuminate their hearts with the brightness of Thy knowledge. I am, O my Lord, Thy servant and the son of Thy servant. I bear witness unto Thy unity, and Thy oneness, and to the sanctity of Thy self and the purity of Thine Essence. Thou beholdest, O my Lord, Thy trusted ones at the mercy of the treacherous among Thy creatures, and the calumniators amidst Thy people. Thou knowest what hath befallen Us at the hands of them whom Thou knowest better than we know them. They have committed what hath torn the veil from such of Thy creatures as are nigh unto Thee. I beseech Thee to assist them to obtain that which hath escaped them in the days of the Dawning-Place of Thy Revelation and the Dayspring of Thine Inspiration. Potent art Thou to do what pleaseth Thee, and in Thy grasp are the reins of all that is in heaven and all that is on earth." The voice and the lamentation of the true Faith have been raised. It calleth aloud and saith: "O people! By the righteousness of God! I have attained unto Him Who hath manifested me and sent me down. This is the Day whereon Sinai hath smiled at Him Who conversed upon it, and Carmel at its Revealer, and the Sadrah at Him Who taught it. Fear ye God, and be not of them that have denied Him. Withhold not yourselves from that which hath been revealed through His grace. Seize ye the living waters of immortality in the name of your Lord, the Lord of all names, and drink ye in the remembrance of Him, Who is the Mighty, the Peerless."

We have, under all circumstances, enjoined on men what is right, and forbidden what is wrong. He Who is the Lord of Being is witness that this Wronged One hath besought from God for His creatures whatever is conducive to unity and harmony, fellowship and concord. By the righteousness of God! This Wronged One is not capable of dissimulation. He, verily, hath revealed that which He desired; He, truly, is the Lord of strength, the Unrestrained.

We once again refer unto some of the sublime words revealed in the Tablet to His Majesty the Sháh, so that thou mayest know of a certainty that whatever hath been mentioned hath come from God: "O King! I was but a man like others, asleep upon My couch, when lo, the breezes of the All-Glorious were wafted over Me, and taught Me the knowledge of all that hath been. This thing is not from Me, but from One Who is Almighty and All-Knowing. And He bade Me lift up My voice between earth and heaven, and for this there befell Me what hath caused the tears of every man of understanding to flow. The learning current amongst men I studied not; their schools I entered not. Ask of the city wherein I dwelt, that thou mayest be well assured that I am not of them who speak falsely. This is but a leaf which the winds of the will of thy Lord, the Almighty, the All-Praised, have stirred. Can it be still when the tempestuous winds are blowing? Nay, by Him Who is the Lord of all Names and Attributes! They move it as they list. The evanescent is as nothing before Him Who is the Ever-Abiding. His all-compelling summons hath reached Me, and caused Me to speak His praise amidst all people. I was indeed as one dead when His behest was uttered. The hand of the will of thy Lord, the Compassionate, the Merciful, transformed Me. Can anyone speak forth of his own accord that for which all men, both high and low, will protest against him? Nay, by Him Who taught the Pen the eternal mysteries, save him whom the grace of the Almighty, the All-Powerful, hath strengthened.

"Look upon this Wronged One, O King, with the eyes of justice; judge thou, then, with truth concerning what hath befallen Him. Of a verity, God hath made thee His shadow amongst men, and the sign of His power unto all that dwell on earth. Judge thou between Us and them that have wronged Us without proof and without an enlightening Book. They that surround thee love thee for their own sakes, whereas this Youth loveth thee for thine own sake, and hath had no desire except to draw thee nigh unto the seat of grace, and to turn thee toward the right-hand of justice. Thy Lord beareth witness unto that which I declare.

"O King! Wert thou to incline thine ears unto the shrill voice of the Pen of Glory and the cooing of the Dove of Eternity, which on the branches of the Lote-Tree beyond which there is no passing, uttereth praises to God, the Maker of all Names and the Creator of earth and heaven, thou wouldst attain unto a station from which thou wouldst behold in the world of being naught save the effulgence of the Adored One, and wouldst regard thy sovereignty as the most contemptible of thy possessions, abandoning it to whosoever might desire it, and setting thy face toward the Horizon aglow with the light of His countenance. Neither wouldst thou ever be willing to bear the burden of dominion save for the purpose of helping thy Lord, the Exalted, the Most High. Then would the Concourse on high bless thee. O how excellent is this most sublime station, couldst thou ascend thereunto through the power of a sovereignty recognized as derived from the Name of God!"

Either thou or someone else hath said: "Let the Súrih of Tawḥíd be translated, so that all may know and be fully persuaded that the one true God begetteth not, nor is He begotten. Moreover, the Bábís believe in his (Bahá'u'lláh's) Divinity and Godhood."

O Shaykh! This station is the station in which one dieth to himself and liveth in God. Divinity, whenever I mention it, indicateth My complete and absolute self-effacement. This is the station in which I have no control over mine own weal or woe nor over my life nor over my resurrection.

O Shaykh! How do the divines of this age account for the effulgent glory which the Sadrah of Utterance hath shed upon the Son of 'Imrán (Moses) on the Sinai of Divine knowledge? He (Moses) hearkened unto the Word which the Burning Bush had uttered, and accepted it; and yet most men are bereft of the power of comprehending this, inasmuch as they have busied themselves with their own concerns, and are unaware of the things which belong unto God. Referring to this, the Siyyid of Findirisk hath well said: "This theme no mortal mind can fathom; be it even that of Abú-Naṣr, or Abú-'Alí Síná (Avicenna)." What explanation can they give concerning that which the Seal of the Prophets (Muḥammad)—may the souls of all else but Him be offered up for His sake—hath said?: "Ye, verily, shall behold your Lord as ye behold the full moon on its fourteenth night." The Commander of the Faithful (Imám ʻAlí)—peace be upon him—moreover, saith in the Khuṭbiy-i-Ṭutunjíyyih: "Anticipate ye the Revelation of Him Who conversed with Moses from the Burning Bush on Sinai." Ḥusayn, the son of ʻAlí—peace be upon him—likewise saith: "Will there be vouchsafed unto anyone besides Thee a Revelation which hath not been vouchsafed unto Thyself—A Revelation Whose Revealer will be He Who revealed Thee. Blind be the eye that seeth Thee not!"

Similar sayings from the Imáms—the blessings of God be upon them—have been recorded and are widely known, and are embodied in books worthy of credence. Blessed is he that perceiveth, and speaketh the pure truth. Well is it with him who, aided by the living waters of the utterance of Him Who is the Desire of all men, hath purified himself from idle fancies and vain imaginings, and torn away, in the name of the All-Possessing, the Most High, the veils of doubt, and renounced the world and all that is therein, and directed himself towards the Most Great Prison.

O Shaykh! No breeze can compare with the breezes of Divine Revelation, whilst the Word which is uttered by God shineth and flasheth as the sun amidst the books of men. Happy the man that hath discovered it, and recognized it, and said: "Praised be Thou, Who art the Desire of the world, and thanks be to Thee, O Well-Beloved of the hearts of such as are devoted to Thee!"

Men have failed to perceive Our purpose in the references We have made to Divinity and Godhood. Were they to apprehend it, they would arise from their places, and cry out: "We, verily, ask pardon of God!" The Seal of the Prophets—may the souls of all else but Him be offered up for His sake—saith: "Manifold are Our relationships with God. At one time, We are He Himself, and He is We Ourself. At another He is that He is, and We are that We are."

Aside from this, why is it that thou didst not mention those other stations which the Abhá Pen hath disclosed? The tongue of this Wronged One hath, many a day and night, given utterance to these sublime words: "O God, my God! I bear witness to Thy unity and Thy oneness, and that Thou art God, and that there is none other God but Thee. Thou hast everlastingly been sanctified above the mention of any one but Thee and the praise of all else except Thyself, and Thou wilt everlastingly continue to be the same as Thou wast from the beginning and hast ever been. I beseech Thee, O King of Eternity, by the Most Great Name, and by the effulgences of the Day-Star of Thy Revelation upon the Sinai of Utterance, and by the billows of the Ocean of Thy knowl-

edge among all created things, to graciously assist Me
in that which will draw Me nigh unto Thee, and
will detach Me from all except Thee. By Thy glory,
O Lord of all being, and the Desire of all creation!
I would love to lay My face upon every single spot
of Thine earth, that perchance it might be honored
by touching a spot ennobled by the footsteps of Thy
loved ones!"

By the righteousness of God! Idle fancies have
debarred men from the Horizon of Certitude, and
vain imaginings withheld them from the Choice
Sealed Wine. In truth I say, and for the sake of God
I declare: This Servant, this Wronged One, is abashed
to claim for Himself any existence whatever, how
much more those exalted grades of being! Every
man of discernment, while walking upon the earth,
feeleth indeed abashed, inasmuch as he is fully aware
that the thing which is the source of his prosperity,
his wealth, his might, his exaltation, his advancement
and power is, as ordained by God, the very earth
which is trodden beneath the feet of all men. There
can be no doubt that whoever is cognizant of this
truth, is cleansed and sanctified from all pride, arro-
gance, and vainglory. Whatever hath been said hath
come from God. Unto this, He, verily, hath borne,
and beareth now, witness, and He, in truth, is the
All-Knowing, the All-Informed.

Beseech God to grant unto men hearing ears, and
sharp sight, and dilated breasts, and receptive hearts,

that haply His servants may attain unto their hearts' Desire, and set their faces towards their Beloved. Troubles, such as no eye hath beheld, have touched this Wronged One. In proclaiming His Cause, He, in no wise, hesitated. Addressing Himself unto the kings and rulers of the earth—may God, exalted be He, assist them—He imparted unto them that which is the cause of the well-being, the unity, the harmony, and the reconstruction of the world, and of the tranquillity of the nations. Among them was Napoleon III, who is reported to have made a certain statement, as a result of which We sent him Our Tablet while in Adrianople. To this, however, he did not reply. After Our arrival in the Most Great Prison there reached Us a letter from his Minister, the first part of which was in Persian, and the latter in his own handwriting. In it he was cordial, and wrote the following: "I have, as requested by you, delivered your letter, and until now have received no answer. We have, however, issued the necessary recommendations to our Minister in Constantinople and our consuls in those regions. If there be anything you wish done, inform us, and we will carry it out."

From his words it became apparent that he understood the purpose of this Servant to have been a request for material assistance. We, therefore, revealed in his (Napoleon III's) name verses in the Súratu'l-Haykal, some of which We now quote, that thou mayest know that the Cause of this Wronged

One hath been revealed for the sake of God, and hath come from Him:

"O King of Paris! Tell the priest to ring the bells no longer. By God, the True One! The Most Mighty Bell hath appeared in the form of Him Who is the Most Great Name, and the fingers of the will of Thy Lord, the Most Exalted, the Most High, toll it out in the heaven of Immortality, in His name, the All-Glorious. Thus have the mighty verses of Thy Lord been again sent down unto thee, that thou mayest arise to remember God, the Creator of earth and heaven, in these days when all the tribes of the earth have mourned, and the foundations of the cities have trembled, and the dust of irreligion hath enwrapped all men, except such as God, the All-Knowing, the All-Wise, was pleased to spare. Say: He Who is the Unconditioned is come, in the clouds of light, that He may quicken all created things with the breezes of His Name, the Most Merciful, and unify the world, and gather all men around this Table which hath been sent down from heaven. Beware that ye deny not the favor of God after it hath been sent down unto you. Better is this for you than that which ye possess; for that which is yours perisheth, whilst that which is with God endureth. He, in truth, ordaineth what He pleaseth. Verily, the breezes of forgiveness have been wafted from the direction of your Lord, the God of Mercy; whoso turneth thereunto, shall be cleansed of his sins, and of all pain and sickness. Happy the man that hath turned towards them, and woe betide him that hath turned aside.

"Wert thou to incline thine inner ear unto all created things, thou wouldst hear: 'The Ancient of Days is come in His great glory!' Everything celebrateth the praise of its Lord. Some have known God and remember Him; others remember Him, yet know Him not. Thus have We set down Our decree in a perspicuous Tablet.

"Give ear, O King, unto the Voice that calleth from the Fire which burneth in this verdant Tree, on this Sinai which hath been raised above the hallowed and snow-white Spot, beyond the Everlasting City; 'Verily, there is none other God but Me, the Ever-Forgiving, the Most Merciful!' We, in truth, have sent Him Whom We aided with the Holy Spirit (Jesus Christ) that He may announce unto you this Light that hath shone forth from the horizon of the will of your Lord, the Most Exalted, the All-Glorious, and Whose signs have been revealed in the West. Set your faces towards Him (Bahá'u'lláh), on this Day which God hath exalted above all other days, and whereon the All-Merciful hath shed the splendor of His effulgent glory upon all who are in heaven and all who are on earth. Arise thou to serve God and help His Cause. He, verily, will assist thee with the hosts of the seen and unseen, and will set thee king over all that whereon the sun riseth. Thy Lord, in truth, is the All-Powerful, the Almighty.

"The breezes of the Most Merciful have passed over all created things; happy the man that hath discovered their fragrance, and set himself towards them with a sound heart. Attire thy temple with the ornament of My Name, and thy tongue with remembrance of Me, and thine heart with love for Me, the Almighty, the Most High. We have desired for thee naught except that which is better for thee than what thou dost possess and all the treasures of the earth. Thy Lord, verily, is knowing, informed of all. Arise, in My Name, amongst My servants, and say: 'O ye peoples of the earth! Turn yourselves towards Him Who hath turned towards you. He, verily, is the Face of God amongst you, and His Testimony and His Guide unto you. He hath come to you with signs which none can produce.' The voice of the Burning Bush is raised in the midmost heart of the world, and the Holy Spirit calleth aloud among the nations: 'Lo, the Desired One is come with manifest dominion!'

"O King! The stars of the heaven of knowledge have fallen, they who seek to establish the truth of My Cause through the things they possess, and who make mention of God in My Name. And yet, when I came unto them in My glory, they turned aside. They, indeed, are of the fallen. This is, truly, that which the Spirit of God (Jesus Christ) hath announced, when He came with truth unto you, He with Whom the Jewish doctors disputed, till at last they perpetrated what hath made the Holy Spirit to lament, and the tears of them that have near access to God to flow.

"Say: O concourse of monks! Seclude not yourselves in your churches and cloisters. Come ye out of them by My leave, and busy, then, yourselves with what will profit you and others. Thus commandeth you He Who is the Lord of the Day of Reckoning. Seclude yourselves in the stronghold of My love. This, truly, is the seclusion that befitteth you, could ye but know it. He that secludeth himself in his house is indeed as one dead. It behooveth man to show forth that which will benefit mankind. He that bringeth forth no fruit is fit for the fire. Thus admonisheth you your Lord; He, verily, is the Mighty, the Bountiful. Enter ye into wedlock, that after you another may arise in your stead. We, verily, have forbidden you lechery, and not that which is conducive to fidelity. Have ye clung unto the promptings of your nature, and cast behind your backs the statutes of God? Fear ye God, and be not of the foolish. But for man, who, on My earth, would remember Me, and how could My attributes and My names be revealed? Reflect, and be not of them that have shut themselves out as by a veil from Him, and were of those that are fast asleep. He that married not (Jesus Christ) could find no place wherein to abide, nor where to lay His head, by reason of what the hands of the treacherous had wrought. His holiness consisted not in the things ye have believed and imagined, but rather in the things which belong unto Us. Ask, that ye may be made aware of His station which hath been exalted above the vain imaginings of all the peoples of the earth. Blessed are they that understand.

"O King! We heard the words thou didst utter in answer to the Czar of Russia, concerning the decision made regarding the war (Crimean War). Thy Lord, verily, knoweth, is informed of all. Thou didst say: 'I lay asleep upon my couch, when the cry of the oppressed, who were drowned in the Black Sea, wakened me.' This is what We heard thee say, and, verily, thy Lord is witness unto what I say. We testify that that which wakened thee was not their cry but the promptings of thine own passions, for We tested thee, and found thee wanting. Comprehend the meaning of My words, and be thou of the discerning. It is not Our wish to address thee words of condemnation, out of regard for the dignity We conferred upon thee in this mortal life. We, verily, have chosen courtesy, and made it the true mark of such as are nigh unto Him. Courtesy is, in truth, a raiment which fitteth all men, whether young or old. Well is it with him that adorneth his temple therewith, and woe unto him who is deprived of this great bounty. Hadst thou been sincere in thy words, thou wouldst have not cast behind thy back the Book of God, when it was sent unto thee by Him

Who is the Almighty, the All-Wise. We have proved thee through it, and found thee other than that which thou didst profess. Arise, and make amends for that which escaped thee. Erelong the world and all that thou possessest will perish, and the kingdom will remain unto God, thy Lord and the Lord of thy fathers of old. It behooveth thee not to conduct thine affairs according to the dictates of thy desires. Fear the sighs of this Wronged One, and shield Him from the darts of such as act unjustly.

"For what thou hast done, thy kingdom shall be thrown into confusion, and thine empire shall pass from thine hands, as a punishment for that which thou hast wrought. Then wilt thou know how thou hast plainly erred. Commotions shall seize all the people in that land, unless thou arisest to help this Cause, and followest Him Who is the Spirit of God (Jesus Christ) in this, the Straight Path. Hath thy pomp made thee proud? By My Life! It shall not endure; nay, it shall soon pass away, unless thou holdest fast by this firm Cord. We see abasement hastening after thee, whilst thou art of the heedless. It behooveth thee when thou hearest His Voice calling from the seat of glory to cast away all that thou possessest, and cry out: 'Here am I, O Lord of all that is in heaven and all that is on earth!'

"O King! We were in 'Iráq, when the hour of parting arrived. At the bidding of the King of Islám (Sultán of Turkey) We set Our steps in his direction.

[51]

Upon Our arrival, there befell Us at the hands of the malicious that which the books of the world can never adequately recount. Thereupon the inmates of Paradise, and they that dwell within the retreats of holiness, lamented; and yet the people are wrapped in a thick veil!"

And further We have said: "More grievous became Our plight from day to day, nay, from hour to hour, until they took Us forth from Our prison and made Us, with glaring injustice, enter the Most Great Prison. And if anyone ask them: 'For what crime were they imprisoned?' they would answer and say: 'They, verily, sought to supplant the Faith with a new religion!' If that which is ancient be what ye prefer, wherefore, then, have ye discarded that which hath been set down in the Torah and the Evangel? Clear it up, O men! By My life! There is no place for you to flee to in this day. If this be My crime, then Muḥammad, the Apostle of God, committed it before Me, and before Him He Who was the Spirit of God (Jesus Christ), and yet earlier He Who conversed with God (Moses). And if My sin be this, that I have exalted the Word of God and revealed His Cause, then indeed am I the greatest of sinners! Such a sin I will not barter for the kingdoms of earth and heaven."

And further We have said: "As My tribulations multiplied, so did My love for God and for His Cause increase, in such wise that all that befell Me from the hosts of the wayward was powerless to deter Me from My purpose. Should they hide Me away in the depths of the earth, yet would they find Me riding aloft on the clouds, and calling out unto God, the Lord of strength and of might. I have offered Myself up in the way of God, and I yearn after tribulations in My love for Him, and for the sake of His good-pleasure. Unto this bear witness the woes which now afflict Me, the like of which no other man hath suffered. Every single hair of Mine head calleth out that which the Burning Bush uttered on Sinai, and each vein of My body invoketh God and saith: 'O would I had been severed in Thy path, so that the world might be quickened, and all its peoples be united!' Thus hath it been decreed by Him Who is the All-Knowing, the All-Informed.

"Know of a truth that your subjects are God's trust amongst you. Watch ye, therefore, over them as ye watch over your own selves. Beware that ye allow not wolves to become the shepherds of the fold, or pride and conceit to deter you from turning unto the poor and the desolate. Arise thou, in My name, above the horizon of renunciation, and set, then, thy face towards the Kingdom, at the bidding of thy Lord, the Lord of strength and of might."

And further We have said: "Adorn the body of Thy kingdom with the raiment of My name, and arise, then, to teach My Cause. Better is this for thee than that which thou possessest. God will, thereby, exalt thy name among all the kings. Potent is He over all things. Walk thou amongst men in the name of God, and by the power of His might, that thou mayest show forth His signs amidst the peoples of the earth."

And further We have said: "Doth it behoove you to relate yourselves to Him Who is the God of mercy, and yet commit the things which the Evil One hath committed? Nay, by the Beauty of Him Who is the All-Glorified! could ye but know it. Purge your hearts from love of the world, and your tongues from calumny, and your limbs from whatsoever may withhold you from drawing nigh unto God, the Mighty, the All-Praised. Say: By the world is meant that which turneth you aside from Him Who is the Dawning-Place of Revelation, and inclineth you unto that which is unprofitable unto you. Verily, the thing that deterreth you, in this day, from God is worldliness in its essence. Eschew it, and approach the Most Sublime Vision, this shining and resplendent Seat. Shed not the blood of anyone, O people, neither judge ye anyone unjustly. Thus have ye been commanded by Him Who knoweth, Who is informed of all. They that commit disorders in the land after it hath been well ordered, these indeed have outstepped the bounds that have been set in the Book. Wretched shall be the abode of the transgressors!"

And further We have said: "Deal not treacherously with the substance of your neighbor. Be ye trustworthy on earth, and withhold not from the poor the things given unto you by God through His grace. He, verily, will bestow upon you the double of what ye possess. He, in truth, is the All-Bounteous, the Most Generous. O people of Bahá! Subdue the citadels of men's hearts with the swords of wisdom and of utterance. They that dispute, as prompted by their desires, are indeed wrapped in a palpable veil. Say: The sword of wisdom is hotter than summer heat, and sharper than blades of steel, if ye do but understand. Draw it forth in My name and through the power of My might, and conquer, then, with it the cities of the hearts of them that have secluded themselves in the stronghold of their corrupt desires. Thus biddeth you the Pen of the All-Glorious, whilst seated beneath the swords of the wayward. If ye become aware of a sin committed by another, conceal it, that God may conceal your own sin. He, verily, is the Concealer, the Lord of grace abounding. O ye rich ones on earth! If ye encounter one who is poor, treat him not disdainfully. Reflect upon that whereof ye were created. Every one of you was created of a sorry germ."

And further We have said: "Regard ye the world as a man's body, which is afflicted with divers ailments, and the recovery of which dependeth upon the harmonizing of all of its component elements. Gather ye around that which We have prescribed unto you, and walk not in the ways of such as create dissension. Meditate on the world and the state of its people. He, for Whose sake the world was called into being, hath been imprisoned in the most desolate of cities ('Akká), by reason of that which the hands of the wayward have wrought. From the horizon of His prison-city He summoneth mankind unto the Dayspring of God, the Exalted, the Great. Exultest thou over the treasures thou dost possess, knowing they shall perish? Rejoicest thou in that thou rulest a span of earth, when the whole world, in the estimation of the people of Bahá, is worth as much as the black in the eye of a dead ant? Abandon it unto such as have set their affections upon it, and turn thou unto Him Who is the Desire of the world. Whither are gone the proud and their palaces? Gaze thou into their tombs, that thou mayest profit by this example, inasmuch as We made it a lesson unto every beholder. Were the breezes of Revelation to seize thee, thou wouldst flee the world, and turn unto the Kingdom, and wouldst expend all thou possessest, that thou mayest draw nigh unto this sublime Vision."

We bade a Christian dispatch this Tablet, and he informed Us that he transmitted both the original and its translation. God, the Almighty, the All-Knowing, hath knowledge of all things.

One of the sections of the Súratu'l-Haykal is the Tablet addressed to His Majesty, the Czar of Russia—may God, exalted and glorified be He—assist him:

"O Czar of Russia! Incline thine ear unto the voice of God, the King, the Holy, and turn thou unto Paradise, the Spot wherein abideth He Who, among the Concourse on high, beareth the most excellent titles, and Who, in the kingdom of creation, is called by the name of God, the Effulgent, the All-Glorious. Beware that nothing deter thee from setting thy face towards thy Lord, the Compassionate, the Most Merciful. We, verily, have heard the thing for which thou didst supplicate thy Lord, whilst secretly communing with Him. Wherefore, the breeze of My loving-kindness wafted forth, and the sea of My mercy surged, and We answered thee in truth. Thy Lord, verily, is the All-Knowing, the All-Wise. Whilst I lay, chained and fettered, in the prison of Ṭihrán, one of thy ministers extended Me his aid. Wherefore hath God ordained for thee a station which the knowledge of none can comprehend except His knowledge. Beware lest thou barter away this sublime station."

And further We have said: "He Who is the Father is come, and the Son (Jesus Christ), in the holy vale, crieth out: 'Here am I, here am I, O Lord, my God!', whilst Sinai circleth round the House, and the Burning Bush calleth aloud: 'The All-Bounteous is come mounted upon the clouds! Blessed is he that draweth nigh unto Him, and woe betide them that are far away.'

"Arise thou amongst men in the name of this all-compelling Cause, and summon, then, the nations unto God, the Mighty, the Great. Be thou not of them who called upon God by one of His names, but who, when He Who is the Object of all names appeared, denied Him and turned aside from Him, and, in the end, pronounced sentence against Him with manifest injustice. Consider and call thou to mind the days whereon the Spirit of God (Jesus Christ) appeared, and Herod gave judgment against Him. God, however, aided Him with the hosts of the unseen, and protected Him with truth, and sent Him down unto another land, according to His promise. He, verily, ordaineth what He pleaseth. Thy Lord truly preserveth whom He willeth, be he in the midst of the seas or in the maw of the serpent, or beneath the sword of the oppressor."

And further We have said: "Again I say: Hearken unto My voice that calleth from My prison, that it may acquaint thee with the things that have befallen My Beauty, at the hands of them that are the manifestations of My glory, and that thou mayest perceive how great hath been My patience, notwithstanding My might, and how immense My forbearance, notwithstanding My power. By My life! Couldst thou but know the things sent down by My Pen, and discover the treasures of My Cause, and the pearls of My mysteries which lie hid in the seas of My names and in the goblets of My words, thou wouldst for longing after His glorious and sublime

Kingdom, lay down thy life in the path of God. Know thou that though My body be beneath the swords of My foes, and My limbs be beset with incalculable afflictions, yet My spirit is filled with a gladness with which all the joys of the earth can never compare."

Likewise, We mention some verses from the Tablet of Her Majesty, the Queen (Queen Victoria)—may God, exalted and glorified be He, assist her. Our purpose is that haply the breezes of Revelation may envelop thee, and cause thee to arise, wholly for the sake of God, and serve His Cause, and that thou mayest transmit any of the Tablets of the kings which might have remained undelivered. This mission is a great mission, and this service a great service. In those regions distinguished divines are numerous, among whom are those Siyyids who are renowned for their eminence and distinction. Confer with them, and show them what hath flowed out of the Pen of Glory, that haply they may be graciously aided to better the condition of the world, and improve the character of peoples of different nations, and may, through the living waters of God's counsels, quench the hatred and the animosity which lie hid and smolder in the hearts of men. We pray God that thou mayest be assisted therein. And this, verily, would not be hard for Him.

"O Queen in London! Incline thine ear unto the voice of thy Lord, the Lord of all mankind, calling from the Divine Lote-Tree: Verily, no God is there but Me, the Almighty, the All-Wise! Cast away all that is on earth, and attire the head of thy kingdom with the crown of the remembrance of Thy Lord, the All-Glorious. He, in truth, hath come unto the world in His most great glory, and all that hath been mentioned in the Gospel hath been fulfilled. The land of Syria hath been honored by the footsteps of its Lord, the Lord of all men, and North and South are both inebriated with the wine of His presence. Blessed is the man that hath inhaled the fragrance of the Most Merciful, and turned unto the Dawning-Place of His beauty, in this resplendent Dawn. The Mosque of Aqsá vibrateth through the breezes of its Lord, the All-Glorious, whilst Batḥá (Mecca) trembleth at the voice of God, the Exalted, the Most High. Every single stone of them celebrateth the praise of the Lord, through this Great Name."

And further We said: "We make mention of thee for the sake of God, and desire that thy name may be exalted through thy remembrance of God, the Creator of earth and of heaven. He, verily, is witness unto that which I say. We have been informed that thou hast forbidden the trading in slaves, both men and women. This, verily, is what God hath enjoined in this wondrous Revelation. God hath, truly, destined a reward for thee, because of this. He, verily, will pay the doer of good, whether man or woman, his due recompense, wert thou to follow what hath been sent unto thee by Him Who is the All-Knowing, the All-Informed. As to him who turneth aside, and swelleth with pride, after that the clear tokens have come unto him, from the Revealer of signs, his work shall God bring to naught. He, in truth, hath power over all things. Man's actions are acceptable after his having recognized (the Manifestation). He that turneth aside from the True One is indeed the most veiled amongst His creatures. Thus hath it been decreed by Him Who is the Almighty, the Most Powerful.

"We have also heard that thou hast entrusted the reins of counsel into the hands of the representatives of the people. Thou, indeed, hast done well, for thereby the foundations of the edifice of thine affairs will be strengthened, and the hearts of all that are beneath thy shadow, whether high or low, will be tranquillized. It behooveth them, however, to be trustworthy among His servants, and to regard themselves as the representatives of all that dwell on earth. This is what counselleth them, in this Tablet, He Who is the Ruler, the All-Wise. And if any one of them directeth himself towards the Assembly, let him turn his eyes unto the Supreme Horizon, and say: 'O my God! I ask Thee, by Thy most glorious Name, to aid me in that which will cause the affairs of Thy servants to prosper, and Thy cities to flourish. Thou, indeed, hast power over all things!' Blessed is he that entereth the Assembly for the sake of God, and judgeth between men with pure justice. He, indeed, is of the blissful.

"O ye members of Assemblies in that land and in other countries! Take ye counsel together, and let your concern be only for that which profiteth mankind, and bettereth the condition thereof, if ye be of them that scan heedfully. Regard the world as the human body which, though at its creation whole and perfect, hath been afflicted, through various causes, with grave disorders and maladies. Not for one day did it gain ease, nay, its sickness waxed more severe, as it fell under the treatment of ignorant physicians, who gave full rein to their personal desires, and have erred grievously. And if at one time, through the care of an able physician, a member of that body was healed, the rest remained afflicted as before. Thus informeth you the All-Knowing, the All-Wise. We behold it, in this day, at the mercy of rulers, so drunk with pride that they cannot discern clearly their own best advantage, much less recognize a Revelation so bewildering and challenging as this."

And further We have said: "That which God hath ordained as the sovereign remedy and mightiest instrument for the healing of the world is the union of all its peoples in one universal Cause, one common Faith. This can in no wise be achieved except through the power of a skilled, an all-powerful, and inspired

Physician. By My life! This is the truth, and all else naught but error. Each time that Most Mighty Instrument hath come, and that Light shone forth from the Ancient Dayspring, He was withheld by ignorant physicians who, even as clouds, interposed themselves between Him and the world. It failed therefore, to recover, and its sickness hath persisted until this day. They indeed were powerless to protect it, or to effect a cure, whilst He Who hath been the Manifestation of Power amongst men was withheld from achieving His purpose, by reason of what the hands of the ignorant physicians have wrought.

"Consider these days in which He Who is the Ancient Beauty hath come in the Most Great Name, that He may quicken the world and unite its peoples. They, however, rose up against Him with sharpened swords, and committed that which caused the Faithful Spirit to lament, until in the end they imprisoned Him in the most desolate of cities, and broke the grasp of the faithful upon the hem of His robe. Were anyone to tell them: 'The World Reformer is come,' they would answer and say: 'Indeed it is proven that He is a fomenter of discord!', and this notwithstanding that they have never associated with Him, and have perceived that He did not seek, for one moment, to protect Himself. At all times He was at the mercy of the wicked doers. At one time they cast Him into prison, at another they banished Him, and at yet another hurried Him from land to land. Thus have they pronounced judgment against Us, and God, truly, is aware of what I say."

This charge of fomenting discord is the same as that imputed aforetime by the Pharaohs of Egypt to Him Who conversed with God (Moses). Read thou what the All-Merciful hath revealed in the Qur'án. He—may He be blessed and glorified—saith: "Moreover We had sent Moses of old with Our signs and with clear authority to Pharaoh, and Hámán, and Qárún: and they said: 'Sorcerer, impostor!' And when He came to them from Our presence with the truth, they said: 'Slay the sons of those who believe as He doth, and save their females alive,' but the stratagem of the unbelievers issued only in failure. And Pharaoh said: 'Let me alone, that I may kill Moses; and let him call upon his Lord: I fear lest he change your religion, or cause disorder to show itself in the land.' And Moses said: 'I take refuge with my Lord, and your Lord from every proud one who believeth not in the Day of Reckoning.'"

Men have, at all times, considered every World Reformer a fomenter of discord, and have referred unto Him in terms with which all are familiar. Each time the Day-Star of Divine Revelation shed its radiance from the horizon of God's Will a great number of men denied Him, others turned aside from Him, and still others calumniated Him, and thereby withheld the servants of God from the river of loving providence of Him Who is the King of creation. In like manner, they who, in this day, have neither met this Wronged One nor associated with Him have said, and even now continue to say, the things thou hast heard and hearest still. Say: "O people! The Sun of Utterance beameth forth in this day, above the horizon of bounty, and the radiance of the Revelation of Him Who spoke on Sinai flasheth and glisteneth before all religions. Purge and sanctify your breasts, and your hearts, and your ears, and your eyes with the living waters of the utterance of the All-Merciful, and set, then, your faces towards Him. By the righteousness of God! Ye shall hear all things proclaim: 'Verily, He the True One is come. Blessed are they that judge with fairness, and blessed they that turn towards Him!'"

Among the things they have imputed to the Divine Lote-Tree (Moses) are charges to the falsity of which every discerning man of knowledge, and every wise and understanding heart, will witness. Thou must, no doubt, have read and considered the verses which have been sent down concerning Him Who conversed with God. He—may He be blessed and glorified—saith: "He said: 'Did We not rear thee among us when a child? And hast thou not passed years of thy life among us? And yet what a deed is that which thou hast done! Thou art one of the ungrateful.' He said: 'I did it indeed, and I was one of those who erred. And I fled from you because I feared you; but My Lord hath given Me wisdom and hath made Me one of His Apostles.' " And elsewhere He—may He be blessed and exalted—saith: "And He entered a city at the time when its inhabitants would not observe Him, and found therein two men fighting, the one, of His own people; the other, of His enemies. And he who was of His own people asked His help against him who was of His enemies. And Moses smote him with His fist and slew him. Said He: 'This is a work of Satan; for he is an enemy, a manifest misleader.' He said: 'O my Lord! I have sinned to mine own hurt, forgive me.' So God forgave Him; for He is the Forgiving, the Merciful. He said: 'Lord! because Thou hast showed me this grace, I will never again be the helper of the wicked.' And in the city at noon He was full of fear, casting furtive glances round Him, and lo, the man whom He had helped the day before, cried out to Him again for help. Said Moses to him: 'Thou art plainly a most depraved person.' And when He would have laid violent hands on him who was their common foe, he said to Him: 'O Moses! Dost Thou desire to slay me, as thou slewest a man yesterday? Thou desirest only to become a tyrant in this land, and desirest not to become a peacemaker.' " Thine ears and thine eyes must needs now be cleansed and sanctified, that thou mayest be able to judge with fairness and justice. Moses Himself, moreover, acknowledged His injustice and waywardness, and testified that fear had seized Him, and that He had transgressed, and fled away. He asked God—exalted be His glory—to forgive Him, and He was forgiven.

O Shaykh! Every time God the True One—exalted be His glory—revealed Himself in the person of His Manifestation, He came unto men with the standard of "He doeth what He willeth, and ordaineth what He pleaseth." None hath the right to ask why or wherefore, and he that doth so, hath indeed turned aside from God, the Lord of Lords. In the days of every Manifestation these things appear and are evident. Likewise, they have said that about this Wronged One, to the falsity of which they who are nigh unto God and are devoted to Him have borne, and still bear, witness. By the righteousness of God! This Hem of His Robe hath ever been and remaineth unsullied, though many have, at the present time, purposed to besmirch it with their lying and unseemly calumnies. God, however, knoweth and they know not. He Who, through the might and power of God, hath arisen before the face of all the kindreds of the earth, and summoned the multitudes to the Supreme Horizon, hath been repudiated by them and they have clung instead unto such men as have invariably withdrawn themselves behind veils and curtains, and busied themselves about their own protection. Moreover, many are now engaged in spreading lies and calumnies, and have no other intention than to instill distrust into the hearts and souls of men. As soon as some one leaveth the Great City (Constantinople) to visit this land, they at once telegraph and proclaim that he hath stolen money and fled to 'Akká. A highly accomplished, learned and distinguished man visited, in his declining years, the Holy Land, seeking peace and retirement, and about him they have written such things as have caused them who are devoted to God and are nigh unto Him to sigh.

His Excellency, the late Mírzá Ḥusayn Khán, Mushíru'd-Dawlih,—may God forgive him—hath known this Wronged One, and he, no doubt, must have given to the Authorities a circumstantial account of the arrival of this Wronged One at the Sublime Porte, and of the things which He said and did. On the day of Our arrival the Government Official, whose duty it was to receive and entertain official visitors, met Us and escorted Us to the place he had been bidden to take Us. In truth, the Government showed these wronged ones the utmost kindness and consideration. The following day Prince Shujá'u'd-Dawlih, accompanied by Mírzá Ṣafá, acting as the representatives of the late Mushíru'd-Dawlih, the Minister (accredited to the Imperial Court) came to visit Us. Others, among whom were several Ministers of the Imperial Government, and including the late Kamál Páshá, likewise called on Us. Wholly reliant on God, and without any reference to any need He might have had, or to any other matter, this Wronged One sojourned for a period of four months in that city. His actions were known and evident unto all, and none can deny them except such as hate Him, and speak not the truth. He that hath recognized God, recognizeth none other but Him. We have never liked, nor like We, to make mention of such things.

Whenever high dignitaries of Persia came to that city (Constantinople) they would exert themselves to the utmost soliciting at every door such allowances and gifts as they might obtain. This Wronged One, however, if He hath done nothing that would redound to the glory of Persia, hath at least acted in a manner that could in no wise disgrace it. That which was done by his late Excellency (Mushíru'd-Dawlih)—may God exalt his station—was not actuated by his friendship towards this Wronged One, but rather was prompted by his own sagacious judgment, and by his desire to accomplish the service he secretly contemplated rendering his Government. I testify that he was so faithful in his service to his Government that dishonesty played no part, and was held in contempt, in the domain of his activities. It was he who was responsible for the arrival of these wronged ones in the Most Great Prison ('Akká). As he was faithful, however, in the discharge of his duty, he deserveth Our commendation. This Wronged One hath, at all times, aimed and striven to exalt and advance the interests of both the government and the people, not to elevate His own station. A number of men have, now, gathered others about them, and have arisen to dishonor this Wronged One. He, nevertheless, beseecheth God—hallowed and glorified be He—to aid them to return unto Him, and assist them to compensate for that which escaped them, and repent before the door of His bounty. He, verily, is the Forgiving, the Merciful.

O Shaykh! My Pen, verily, lamenteth over Mine own Self, and My Tablet weepeth sore over what hath befallen Me at the hands of one (Mírzá Yaḥyá) over whom We watched for successive years, and who, day and night, served in My presence, until he was made to err by one of My servants, named Siyyid Muḥammad. Unto this bear witness My believing servants who accompanied Me in My exile from Baghdád to this, the Most Great Prison. And there befell Me at the hands of both of them that which made every man of understanding to cry out, and he who is endued with insight to groan aloud, and the tears of the fair-minded to flow.

We pray to God to graciously assist them that have been led astray to be just and fair-minded, and to make them aware of that whereof they have been heedless. He, in truth, is the All-Bounteous, the Most Generous. Debar not Thy servants, O my Lord, from the door of Thy grace, and drive them not away from the court of Thy presence. Assist them to dispel the mists of idle fancy, and to tear away the veils of vain imaginings and hopes. Thou art, verily, the All-Possessing, the Most High. No God is there but Thee, the Almighty, the Gracious.

I swear by the Day-Star of God's Testimony that hath shone from the horizon of certitude! This Wronged One, in the day-time and in the night-season, occupied Himself with that which would edify the souls of men, until the light of knowledge prevailed over the darkness of ignorance.

O Shaykh! Time and again have I declared, and now yet again I affirm, that for two score years We have, through the grace of God and by His irresistible and potent will, extended such aid to His Majesty the Sháh—may God assist him—as the exponents of justice and of equity would regard as incontestable and absolute. None can deny it, unless he be a transgressor and sinner, or one who would hate Us or doubt Our truth. How very strange that until now the Ministers of State and the representatives of the people have alike remained unaware of such conspicuous and undeniable service, and, if apprized of it, have, for reasons of their own, chosen to ignore it! Previous to these forty years controversies and conflicts continually prevailed and agitated the servants of God. But since then, aided by the hosts of wisdom, of utterance, of exhortations and understanding, they have all seized and taken fast hold of the firm cord of patience and of the shining hem of fortitude, in such wise that this wronged people endured steadfastly whatever befell them, and committed everything unto God, and this notwithstanding that in Mázindarán and at Rasht a great many have been most hideously tormented. Among them was his honor, Ḥájí Naṣír, who, unquestionably, was a brilliant light that shone forth above the horizon of resignation. After he had suffered martyrdom, they plucked out his eyes and cut off his nose, and inflicted on him such indignities that strangers wept and lamented, and secretly raised funds to support his wife and children.

O Shaykh! My Pen is abashed to recount what actually took place. In the land of Ṣád (Iṣfahán) the fire of tyranny burned with such a hot flame that every fair-minded person groaned aloud. By thy life! The cities of knowledge and of understanding wept with such a weeping that the souls of the pious and of the God-fearing were melted. The twin shining lights, Ḥasan and Ḥusayn (The King of Martyrs and the Beloved of Martyrs) offered up spontaneously their lives in that city. Neither fortune, nor wealth, nor glory, could deter them! God knoweth the things which befell them and yet the people are, for the most part, unaware!

Before them one named Kázim and they who were with him, and after them, his honor Ashraf, all quaffed the draught of martyrdom with the utmost fervor and longing, and hastened unto the Supreme Companion. In like manner, at the time

of Sardár 'Azíz <u>Kh</u>án, that godly man, Mírzá
Muṣṭafá, and his fellow-martyrs, were arrested, and
despatched unto the Supreme Friend in the All-
Glorious Horizon. Briefly, in every city the evidences
of a tyranny, beyond like or equal, were unmis-
takably clear and manifest, and yet none arose in self-
defence! Call thou to mind his honor Badí', who was
the bearer of the Tablet to His Majesty the <u>Sh</u>áh,
and reflect how he laid down his life. That knight,
who spurred on his charger in the arena of renunciation, threw down the precious crown of life for
the sake of Him Who is the Incomparable Friend.

O <u>Sh</u>ay<u>kh</u>! If things such as these are to be denied,
what shall, then, be deemed worthy of credence?
Set forth the truth, for the sake of God, and be not
of them that hold their peace. They arrested his
honor Najaf-'Alí, who hastened, with rapture and
great longing, unto the field of martyrdom, uttering
these words: "We have kept both Bahá and the
<u>kh</u>ún-bahá (bloodmoney)!" With these words he
yielded up his spirit. Meditate on the splendor and
glory which the light of renunciation, shining from
the upper chamber of the heart of Mullá 'Alí-Ján,
hath shed. He was so carried away by the breezes of
the Most Sublime Word and by the power of the
Pen of Glory that to him the field of martyrdom
equalled, nay outrivalled, the haunts of earthly de-
lights. Ponder upon the conduct of 'Abá-Baṣír and
Siyyid A<u>sh</u>raf-i-Zanjání. They sent for the mother

of Ashraf to dissuade her son from his purpose. But she spurred him on until he suffered a most glorious martyrdom.

O Shaykh! This people have passed beyond the narrow straits of names, and pitched their tents upon the shores of the sea of renunciation. They would willingly lay down a myriad lives, rather than breathe the word desired by their enemies. They have clung to that which pleaseth God, and are wholly detached and freed from the things which pertain unto men. They have preferred to have their heads cut off rather than utter one unseemly word. Ponder this in thine heart. Methinks they have quaffed their fill of the ocean of renunciation. The life of the present world hath failed to withhold them from suffering martyrdom in the path of God.

In Mázindarán a vast number of the servants of God were exterminated. The Governor, under the influence of calumniators, robbed a great many of all that they possessed. Among the charges he laid against them was that they had been laying up arms, whereas upon investigation it was found out that they had nothing but an unloaded rifle! Gracious God! This people need no weapons of destruction, inasmuch as they have girded themselves to recon-struct the world. Their hosts are the hosts of goodly deeds, and their arms the arms of upright conduct, and their commander the fear of God. Blessed that one that judgeth with fairness. By the righteousness of God! Such hath been the patience, the calm, the resignation and contentment of this people that they have become the exponents of justice, and so great hath been their forbearance, that they have suffered themselves to be killed rather than kill, and this notwithstanding that these whom the world hath wronged have endured tribulations the like of which the history of the world hath never recorded, nor the eyes of any nation witnessed. What is it that could have induced them to reconcile themselves to these grievous trials, and to refuse to put forth a hand to repel them? What could have caused such resignation and serenity? The true cause is to be found in the ban which the Pen of Glory hath, day and night, chosen to impose, and in Our assumption of the reins of authority, through the power and might of Him Who is the Lord of all mankind.

Remember the father of Badí'. They arrested that wronged one, and ordered him to curse and revile his Faith. He, however, through the grace of God and the mercy of his Lord, chose martyrdom, and attained thereunto. If ye would reckon up the martyrs in the path of God, ye could not count them. Consider his honor Siyyid Ismá'íl—upon him be the peace of God, and His loving-kindness—how, before daybreak he was wont to dust, with his own turban, the doorstep of My house, and in the end, whilst standing on the banks of the river, with his eyes fixed on that same house, offered up, by his own hand, his life.

Do thou ponder on the penetrative influence of

the Word of God. Every single one of these souls was first ordered to blaspheme and curse his faith, yet none was found to prefer his own will to the Will of God.

O Shaykh! In former times he that was chosen to be slain was but one person, whereas now this Wronged One hath produced for thee that which causeth every fair-minded man to marvel. Judge fairly, I adjure thee, and arise to serve thy Lord. He, verily, shall reward thee with a reward which neither the treasures of the earth nor all the possessions of kings and rulers can equal. In all thine affairs put thy reliance in God, and commit them unto Him. He will render thee a reward which the Book hath ordained as great. Occupy thyself, during these fleeting days of thy life, with such deeds as will diffuse the fragrance of Divine good-pleasure, and will be adorned with the ornament of His acceptance. The acts of his honor, Balál, the Ethiopian, were so acceptable in the sight of God that the "sín" of his stuttering tongue excelled the "shín" pronounced by all the world. This is the day whereon all peoples should shed the light of unity and concord. In brief, the pride and vanity of certain of the peoples of the world have made havoc of true understanding, and laid waste the home of justice and of equity.

O Shaykh! That which hath touched this Wronged One is beyond compare or equal. We have borne it all with the utmost willingness and resignation, so that the souls of men may be edified, and the Word of God be exalted. While confined in the prison of the Land of Mím (Mázindarán) We were one day delivered into the hands of the divines. Thou canst well imagine what befell Us. Shouldst thou at some time happen to visit the dungeon of His Majesty the Sháh, ask the director and chief jailer to show thee those two chains, one of which is known as Qará-Guhar, and the other as Salásil. I swear by the Day-Star of Justice that for four months this Wronged One was tormented and chained by one or the other of them. "My grief exceedeth all the woes to which Jacob gave vent, and all the afflictions of Job are but a part of My sorrows!"

Likewise, ponder thou upon the martyrdom of Hájí Muhammad-Ridá in the City of Love ('Ishqábád). The tyrants of the earth have subjected that wronged one to such trials as have caused many foreigners to weep and lament for, as reported and ascertained, no less than thirty-two wounds were inflicted upon his blessed body. Yet none of the faithful transgressed My commandment, nor raised his hand in resistance. Come what might, they refused to allow their own inclinations to supersede that which the Book hath decreed, though a considerable number of this people have resided, and still reside, in that city.

We entreat His Majesty the Sháh,—may God, hallowed and glorified be He, assist him—himself to

ponder upon these things, and to judge with equity
and justice. Although in recent years a number of
the faithful have, in most of the cities of Persia, suffered themselves to be killed rather than kill, yet the
hatred smouldering in certain hearts hath blazed
more fiercely than before. For the victims of oppression to intercede in favor of their enemies is, in
the estimation of rulers, a princely deed. Some must
have certainly heard that this oppressed people have,
in that city ('Ishqábád), pleaded with the Governor
on behalf of their murderers, and asked for the miti-
gation of their sentence. Take, then, good heed, ye
who are men of insight!

O Shaykh! These perspicuous verses have been
sent down in one of the Tablets by the Abhá Pen:
"Hearken, O servant, unto the voice of this Wronged
One, Who hath endured grievous vexations and trials
in the path of God, the Lord of all Names, until
such time as He was cast into prison, in the Land of
Ṭá (Ṭihrán). He summoned men unto the most
sublime Paradise, and yet they seized Him and
paraded Him through cities and countries. How
many the nights during which slumber fled from the
eyes of My loved ones, because of their love for Me;
and how numerous the days whereon I had to face
the assaults of the peoples against Me! At one time
I found Myself on the heights of mountains; at another in the depths of the prison of Ṭá (Ṭihrán), in
chains and fetters. By the righteousness of God!

I was at all times thankful unto Him, uttering His praise, engaged in remembering Him, directed towards Him, satisfied with His pleasure, and lowly and submissive before Him. So passed My days, until they ended in this Prison ('Akká) which hath made the earth to tremble and the heavens to sigh. Happy that one who hath cast away his vain imaginings, when He Who was hid came with the standards of His signs. We, verily, have announced unto men this Most Great Revelation, and yet the people are in a state of strange stupor."

Thereupon, a Voice was raised from the direction of Ḥijáz, calling aloud and saying: "Great is thy blessedness, O 'Akká, in that God hath made thee the dayspring of His Most Sweet Voice, and the dawn of His most mighty signs. Happy art thou in that the Throne of Justice hath been established upon thee, and the Day-Star of God's loving-kindness and bounty hath shone forth above thy horizon. Well is it with every fair-minded person that hath judged fairly Him Who is the Most Great Remembrance, and woe betide him that hath erred and doubted."

Following upon the death of some of the martyrs, the Lawḥ-i-Burhán (Tablet of the Proof) was sent down from the heaven of the Revelation of Him Who is the Lord of Religions:

"He is the Almighty, the All-Knowing, the All-Wise! The winds of hatred have encompassed the Ark of Baṭḥá (Mecca), by reason of that which the

[79]

hands of the oppressors have wrought. O thou who art reputed for thy learning! Thou hast pronounced sentence against them for whom the books of the world have wept, and in whose favor the scriptures of all religions have testified. Thou, who art gone far astray, art indeed wrapt in a thick veil. By God Himself! Thou hast pronounced judgment against them through whom the horizon of faith hath been illumined. Unto this bear witness They Who are the Dawning-Places of Revelation and the Manifestations of the Cause of thy Lord, the Most Merciful, Who have sacrificed Their souls and all that They possessed in His straight Path. The Faith of God hath cried everywhere, by reason of thy tyranny, and yet thou disportest thyself and art of them that exult. There is no hatred in Mine heart for thee nor for anyone. Every man of discernment beholdeth thee, and such as are like thee, engulfed in evident folly. Hadst thou realized that which thou hast done, thou wouldst have cast thyself into the fire, or abandoned thine home and fled unto the mountains, or wouldst have groaned until thou hadst returned unto the place destined for thee by Him Who is the Lord of strength and of might. O thou who art even as nothing! Rend thou asunder the veils of idle fancies and vain imaginings, that thou mayest behold the Day-Star of knowledge shining from this resplendent Horizon. Thou hast torn in pieces a remnant of the Prophet Himself, and imagined that thou hadst helped the Faith of God. Thus hath thy soul prompted thee, and thou art truly one of the heedless. Thine act hath consumed the hearts of the Concourse on high, and those of such as have circled round the Cause of God, the Lord of the worlds. The soul of the Chaste One (Fáṭimih) melted, by reason of thy cruelty, and the inmates of Paradise wept sore in that blessed Spot.

"Judge thou fairly, I adjure thee by God. What proof did the Jewish doctors adduce wherewith to condemn Him Who was the Spirit of God (Jesus Christ), when He came unto them with truth? What could have been the evidence produced by the Pharisees and the idolatrous priests to justify their denial of Muḥammad, the Apostle of God when He came unto them with a Book that judged between truth and falsehood with a justice which turned into light the darkness of the earth, and enraptured the hearts of such as had known Him? Indeed thou hast produced, in this day, the same proofs which the foolish divines advanced in that age. Unto this testifieth He Who is the King of the realm of grace in this great Prison. Thou hast, truly, walked in their ways, nay, hast surpassed them in their cruelty, and hast deemed thyself to be helping the Faith and defending the Law of God, the All-Knowing, the All-Wise. By Him Who is the Truth! Thine iniquity hath made Gabriel to groan, and hath drawn tears from the Law of God, through which the breezes of justice have been wafted over all who are in heaven and on earth. Hast thou fondly imagined that the judgment thou didst pronounce hath profited thee? Nay, by Him Who is the King of all Names! Unto thy loss testifieth He with Whom is the knowledge of all things as recorded in the preserved Tablet.

"O thou who hast gone astray! Thou hast neither seen Me, nor associated with Me, nor been My companion for the fraction of a moment. How is it, then, that thou hast bidden men to curse Me? Didst thou, in this, follow the promptings of thine own desires, or didst thou obey thy Lord? Produce thou a sign, if thou art one of the truthful. We testify that thou hast cast behind thy back the Law of God, and laid hold on the dictates of thy passions. Nothing, in truth, escapeth His knowledge; He, verily, is the Incomparable, the All-Informed. O heedless one! Hearken unto that which the Merciful hath revealed in the Qur'án: 'Say not to every one who meeteth you with a greeting, "Thou art not a believer." ' Thus hath He decreed in Whose grasp are the kingdoms of Revelation and of creation, if thou be of them that hearken. Thou hast set aside the commandment of God, and clung unto the promptings of thine own desire. Woe, then, unto thee, O careless one that doubtest! If thou deniest Me, by what proof canst thou vindicate the truth of that which thou dost possess? Produce it, then, O thou who hast joined partners with God, and turned aside from His sovereignty that hath encompassed the worlds!

"Know thou that he is truly learned who hath acknowledged My Revelation, and drunk from the Ocean of My knowledge, and soared in the atmosphere of My love, and cast away all else besides Me, and taken firm hold on that which hath been sent down from the Kingdom of My wondrous utterance. He, verily, is even as an eye unto mankind, and as the spirit of life unto the body of all creation. Glorified be the All-Merciful Who hath enlightened him, and caused him to arise and serve His great and mighty Cause. Verily, such a man is blessed by the Concourse on high, and by them who dwell within the Tabernacle of Grandeur, who have quaffed My sealed Wine in My Name, the Omnipotent, the All-Powerful. If thou be of them that occupy such a sublime station, produce then a sign from God, the Creator of the heavens. And shouldst thou recognize thy powerlessness, do thou rein in thy passions, and return unto thy Lord, that perchance He may forgive thee thy sins which have caused the leaves of the Divine Lote-Tree to be burnt up, and the Rock to cry out, and the eyes of men of understanding to weep. Because of thee the Veil of Divinity was rent asunder, and the Ark has foundered, and the She-Camel was hamstrung, and the Spirit (Jesus) groaned in His sublime retreat. Disputest thou with Him

Who hath come unto thee with the testimonies of God and His signs which thou possessest and which are in the possession of them that dwell on earth? Open thine eyes that thou mayest behold this Wronged One shining forth above the horizon of the will of God, the Sovereign, the Truth, the Resplendent. Unstop, then, the ear of thine heart that thou mayest hearken unto the speech of the Divine Lote-Tree that hath been raised up in truth by God, the Almighty, the Beneficent. Verily, this Tree, notwithstanding the things that befell it by reason of thy cruelty and of the transgressions of such as are like thee, calleth aloud and summoneth all men unto the Sadratu'l-Muntahá and the Supreme Horizon. Blessed is the soul that hath gazed on the Most Mighty Sign, and the ear that hath heard His most sweet Voice, and woe to whosoever hath turned aside and done wickedly.

"O thou who hast turned away from God! Wert thou to look with the eye of fairness upon the Divine Lote-Tree, thou wouldst perceive the marks of thy sword on its boughs, and its branches, and its leaves, notwithstanding that God created thee for the purpose of recognizing and of serving it. Reflect, that haply thou mayest recognize thine iniquity and be numbered with such as have repented. Thinkest thou that We fear thy cruelty? Know thou and be well assured that from the first day whereon the voice of the Most Sublime Pen was raised betwixt earth and heaven We offered up Our souls, and Our bodies, and Our sons, and Our possessions in the path of God, the Exalted, the Great, and We glory therein amongst all created things and the Concourse on high. Unto this testify the things which have befallen Us in this straight Path. By God! Our hearts were consumed, and Our bodies were crucified, and Our blood was spilt, while Our eyes were fixed on the horizon of the loving-kindness of their Lord, the Witness, the All-Seeing. The more grievous their woes, the greater waxed the love of the people of Bahá. Unto their sincerity hath borne witness what the All-Merciful hath sent down in the Qur'án. He saith: 'Wish ye, then, for death, if ye are sincere.' Who is to be preferred, he that hath sheltered himself behind curtains, or he that hath offered himself in the path of God? Judge thou fairly, and be not of them that rove distraught in the wilderness of falsehood. So carried away have they been by the living waters of the love of the Most Merciful, that neither the arms of the world nor the swords of the nations have deterred them from setting their faces towards the ocean of the bounty of their Lord, the Giver, the Generous.

"By God! Troubles have failed to unnerve Me, and the repudiation of the divines hath been powerless to weaken Me. I have spoken, and still speak forth before the face of men: 'The door of grace hath been unlocked and He Who is the Dayspring of

Justice is come with perspicuous signs and evident testimonies, from God, the Lord of strength and of might!' Present thyself before Me that thou mayest hear the mysteries which were heard by the Son of 'Imrán (Moses) upon the Sinai of Wisdom. Thus commandeth thee He Who is the Dawning-Place of the Revelation of thy Lord, the God of Mercy, from His great Prison."

Thereupon hath the cry and the lamentation of the true Faith been raised once again, saying: "Verily, Sinai calleth aloud and saith: 'O people of the Bayán! Fear ye the Merciful. Indeed have I attained unto Him Who conversed upon me, and the ecstasies of my joy have seized the pebbles of the earth and the dust thereof.' And the Bush exclaimeth: 'O people of the Bayán! Judge ye fairly that which hath in truth been manifested. Verily the Fire which God revealed unto the One Who conversed with Him is now manifested. Unto this beareth witness every man of insight and understanding.' "

We have made mention of certain martyrs of this Revelation, and have likewise cited some of the verses which were sent down concerning them from the kingdom of Our utterance. We fain would hope that, rid of all attachment to the world, thou wilt ponder the things which We have mentioned.

It behooveth thee now to reflect upon the state of Mírzá Hádí Dawlat-Ábádí and of Ṣád-i-Iṣfahání (Ṣadru'l-'Ulamá), who reside in the Land of Ṭá

(Ṭihrán). No sooner had the former heard that he had been called a Bábí than he became so perturbed that his poise and dignity forsook him. He ascended the pulpits and spoke words which ill befitted him. From time immemorial the clay clods of the world have, wholly by reason of their love of leadership, perpetrated such acts as have caused men to err. Thou must not, however, imagine that all the faithful are such as these two. We have described unto thee the constancy, the firmness, the steadfastness, the certitude, the imperturbability and the dignity of the martyrs of this Revelation, that thou mayest be well-informed. My purpose in citing the passages from the Tablets to the kings and others hath been that thou mayest know of a certainty that this Wronged One hath not concealed the Cause of God, but hath proclaimed and delivered, in the most eloquent language, before the face of the world, the things He had been commissioned to set forth. Certain faint-hearted ones, however, such as Hádí and others, have tampered with the Cause of God and have, in their concern for this fleeting life, said and done that which caused the eye of justice to weep and the Pen of Glory to groan, notwithstanding their ignorance of the essentials of this Cause; whereas this Wronged One hath revealed it for the sake of God.

O Hádí! Thou hast gone unto My brother and hast seen him. Set now thy face towards the court of this Wronged One, that haply the breezes of Revelation and the breaths of inspiration may assist thee and enable thee to attain thy goal. Whoever gazeth this day on My signs will distinguish truth from false-hood as the sun from shadow, and will be made cognizant of the goal. God is aware and beareth Me witness that whatever hath been mentioned was for the sake of God, that haply thou mayest be the cause of the guidance of men, and mayest deliver the peoples of the world from idle fancies and vain imaginings. Gracious God! Until now they that have turned aside and denied Me have failed to recognize Who despatched that which was delivered unto the Herald—the Primal Point! The knowledge of it is with God, the Lord of the worlds.

Exert thyself, O Shaykh, and arise to serve this Cause. The Sealed Wine is disclosed in this day before the faces of men. Seize it in the name of thy Lord, and quaff thy fill in remembrance of Him Who is the Mighty, the Incomparable. Night and day hath this Wronged One been occupied in that which would unite the hearts, and edify the souls of men. The events that have happened in Persia during the early years have truly saddened the well-favored and sincere ones. Each year witnessed a fresh massacre, pillage, plunder, and shedding of blood. At one time there appeared in Zanján that which caused the greatest consternation; at another in Nayríz, and at yet another in Ṭabarsí, and finally there occurred the episode of the Land of Ṭá (Ṭihrán). From that time onwards this Wronged One, assisted by the One True God—exalted be His glory—acquainted this oppressed people with the things which beseemed them. All have sanctified themselves from the things which they and others possess, and have clung unto, and fixed their eyes upon that which pertaineth unto God.

It is now incumbent upon His Majesty the Sháh—may God, exalted be He, protect him—to deal with this people with loving-kindness and mercy. This Wronged One pledgeth Himself, before the Divine Kaaba, that, apart from truthfulness and trustworthiness, this people will show forth nothing that can in any way conflict with the world-adorning views of His Majesty. Every nation must have a high regard for the position of its sovereign, must be submissive unto him, must carry out his behests, and hold fast his authority. The sovereigns of the earth have been and are the manifestations of the power, the grandeur and the majesty of God. This Wronged One hath at no time dealt deceitfully with anyone. Every one is well aware of this, and beareth witness unto it. Regard for the rank of sovereigns is divinely ordained, as is clearly attested by the words of the Prophets of God and His chosen ones. He Who is the Spirit (Jesus)—may peace be upon Him—was asked: "O Spirit of God! Is it lawful to give tribute to Caesar or not?" And He made reply: "Yea, render to Caesar the things that are Caesar's and to God the things that are God's." He forbade it not. These two sayings are, in the estimation of men of insight, one and the same, for if that which belonged to Caesar had not come from God, He would have forbidden it. And likewise in the sacred verse: "Obey God and obey the Apostle, and those among you invested with authority." By "those invested with authority" is meant primarily and more especially the Imáms—the blessings of God rest upon them! They, verily, are the manifestations of the power of God, and the sources of His authority, and the repositories of His knowledge, and the daysprings of His commandments. Secondarily these words refer unto the kings and rulers—those through the brightness of whose justice the horizons of the world are resplendent and luminous. We fain would hope that His Majesty the Sháh will shine forth with a light of justice whose radiance will envelop all the kindreds of the earth. It is incumbent upon every one to beseech the one true God on his behalf for that which is meet and seemly in this day.

O God, my God, and my Master, and my Mainstay, and my Desire, and my Beloved! I ask Thee by the mysteries which were hid in Thy knowledge, and by the signs which have diffused the fragrance of Thy loving-kindness, and by the billows of the ocean of Thy bounty, and by the heaven of Thy grace and generosity, and by the blood spilt in Thy path, and by the hearts consumed in their love for

Thee, to assist His Majesty the Sháh with Thy power and Thy sovereignty, that from him may be manifested that which will everlastingly endure in Thy Books, and Thy Scriptures, and Thy Tablets. Hold Thou his hand, O my Lord, with the hand of Thine omnipotence, and illuminate him with the light of Thy knowledge, and adorn him with the adornment of Thy virtues. Potent art Thou to do what pleaseth Thee, and in Thy grasp are the reins of all created things. No God is there but Thee, the Ever-Forgiving, the All-Bounteous.

In the Epistle to the Romans Saint Paul hath written: "Let every soul be subject unto the higher powers. For there is no power but of God; the powers that be are ordained of God. Whosoever therefore resisteth the power, resisteth the ordinance of God." And further: "For he is the minister of God, a revenger to execute wrath upon him that doeth evil." He saith that the appearance of the kings, and their majesty and power are of God.

Moreover, in the traditions of old, references have been made which the divines have seen and heard. We beseech God—blessed and glorified be He—to aid thee, O Shaykh, to lay fast hold on that which hath been sent down from the heaven of the bounty of God, the Lord of the worlds. The divines must needs unite with His Majesty, the Sháh, and cleave unto that which will insure the protection, the security, the welfare and prosperity of men. A just king enjoyeth nearer access unto God than anyone. Unto this testifieth He Who speaketh in His Most Great Prison. God! There is none other God but Him, the One, the Incomparable, the Almighty, the All-Knowing, the All-Wise.

Wert thou, for the sake of God, to ponder, though it be but for an hour, upon the things which have occurred in former times and more recently, thou wouldst turn away from the things thou dost possess unto the things which belong unto God, and wouldst become a means for the exaltation of His Word. Hath, from the foundation of the world until the present day, any Light or Revelation shone forth from the dayspring of the will of God which the kindreds of the earth have accepted, and Whose Cause they have acknowledged? Where is it to be found, and what is its name? Since the Seal of the Prophets (Muḥammad)—may all else but Him be His sacrifice—and before Him the Spirit of God (Jesus), as far back as the First Manifestation, all have at the time of Their appearance suffered grievously. Some were held to be possessed, others were called impostors, and were treated in a manner that the pen is ashamed to describe. By God! There befell Them what hath made all created things to sigh, and yet the people are, for the most part, sunk in manifest ignorance! We pray God to assist them to return unto Him, and to repent before the door of His mercy. Potent is He over all things.

At this moment the shrill voice of the Most Sublime Pen hath been raised, and hath addressed Me saying: "Admonish the Shaykh even as Thou hast admonished one of Thy Branches (sons), that haply the breezes of Thine utterance may attract and draw him nigh unto God, the Lord of the worlds."

"Be generous in prosperity, and thankful in adversity. Be worthy of the trust of thy neighbor, and look upon him with a bright and friendly face. Be a treasure to the poor, an admonisher to the rich, an answerer to the cry of the needy, a preserver of the sanctity of thy pledge. Be fair in thy judgment, and guarded in thy speech. Be unjust to no man, and show all meekness to all men. Be as a lamp unto them that walk in darkness, a joy to the sorrowful, a sea for the thirsty, a haven for the distressed, an upholder and defender of the victim of oppression. Let integrity and uprightness distinguish all thine acts. Be a home for the stranger, a balm to the suffering, a tower of strength for the fugitive. Be eyes to the blind, and a guiding light unto the feet of the erring. Be an ornament to the countenance of truth, a crown to the brow of fidelity, a pillar of the temple of righteousness, a breath of life to the body of mankind, an ensign of the hosts of justice, a luminary above the horizon of virtue, a dew to the soil of the human heart, an ark on the ocean of knowledge, a sun in the heaven of bounty, a gem on the diadem of wisdom, a shining light in the firmament of thy generation, a fruit upon the tree of humility. We pray God to protect thee from the heat of jealousy and the cold of hatred. He verily is nigh, ready to answer." Thus hath My tongue spoken unto one of My Branches (sons), and We have mentioned it unto such of Our loved ones as have cast away their idle fancies, and clung unto that which hath been prescribed unto them in the day whereon the Day-Star of Certitude hath shone forth above the horizon of the will of God, the Lord of the worlds. This is the day on which the Bird of Utterance hath warbled its melody upon the branches, in the name of its Lord, the God of Mercy. Blessed is the man that hath, on the wings of longing, soared towards God, the Lord of the Judgment Day.

The one true God well knoweth, and all the company of His trusted ones testify, that this Wronged One hath, at all times, been faced with dire peril. But for the tribulations that have touched Me in the path of God, life would have held no sweetness for Me, and My existence would have profited Me nothing. For them who are endued with discernment, and whose eyes are fixed upon the Sublime Vision, it is no secret that I have been, most of the days of My life, even as a slave, sitting under a sword hanging on a thread, knowing not whether it would fall soon or late upon him. And yet, notwithstanding all this We render thanks unto God, the Lord of the worlds. Mine inner tongue reciteth, in the day-time and in the night-season, this prayer: "Glory to Thee, O my God! But for the tribulations which are sustained in Thy path, how could Thy true lovers be recognized; and were it not for the trials which are borne for love of Thee, how could the station of such as yearn for Thee be revealed? Thy might beareth Me witness! The companions of all who adore Thee are the tears they shed, and the comforters of such as seek Thee are the groans they utter, and the food of them who haste to meet Thee is the fragments of their broken hearts. How sweet to my taste is the bitterness of death suffered in Thy path, and how precious in my estimation are the shafts of Thine enemies when encountered for the sake of the exaltation of Thy Word! Let me quaff in Thy Cause, O my God and my Master, whatsoever Thou didst desire, and send down upon me in Thy love all Thou didst ordain. By Thy glory! I wish only what Thou wishest, and cherish what Thou cherishest. In Thee have I, at all times, placed My whole trust and confidence. Thou art verily the All-Possessing, the Most High. Raise up, I implore Thee, O my God, as helpers to this Revelation such as shall be counted worthy of Thy Name and of Thy sovereignty, that they may remember Thee among Thy creatures, and hoist the ensigns of Thy victory in Thy land, and adorn them with Thy virtues and Thy commandments. No God is there but Thee, the Help in Peril, the Self-Subsisting."

Thereupon the voice of the true Faith was lifted up, calling aloud again and again and saying: "O concourse of the earth! By God! I am the true Faith of God amongst you. Beware that ye deny Me not. God hath manifested Me with a light that hath encompassed all that are in the heavens and all that are on earth. Judge ye equitably, O people, My manifestation, and the revelation of My glory, and the radiance of My light, and be not of them that act unjustly."

O Shaykh! This Wronged One beseecheth God—blessed and glorified be He—to make thee the one who will open the door of justice, and reveal through thee His Cause among His servants. He, verily, is the All-Powerful, the Almighty, the All-Bounteous.

O Shaykh! Entreat thou the one true God to sanctify the ears, and the eyes, and the hearts of mankind, and to protect them from the desires of a corrupt inclination. For malice is a grievous malady which depriveth man from recognizing the Great Being, and debarreth him from the splendors of the sun of certitude. We pray and hope that through the grace and mercy of God He may remove this mighty obstacle. He, verily, is the Potent, the All-Subduing, the Almighty.

At this moment a Voice was raised from the right-hand of the Luminous Spot: "God! There is none other God but Him, the Ordainer, the All-Wise! Recite Thou unto the Shaykh the remaining passages of the Lawḥ-i-Burhán (Tablet of the Proof) that they may draw him unto the horizon of the Revelation of his Lord, the God of Mercy, that haply he may arise to aid My Cause with perspicuous signs and exalted testimonies, and may speak forth amongst men that which the Tongue of Testimony hath spoken: 'The Kingdom is God's, the Lord of the worlds!' "

"Peruse thou the Kitáb-i-Íqán (Book of Certitude) and that which the All-Merciful hath sent down unto the King of Paris (Napoleon III) and to such as are like him, that thou mayest be made aware of the things that have happened in the past, and be persuaded that We have not sought to spread disorder in the land after it had been well-ordered. We exhort, wholly for the sake of God, His servants. Let him who wisheth turn unto Him, and him who wisheth turn aside. Our Lord, the Merciful, is verily the All-Sufficing, the All-Praised. O concourse of the kindreds of the earth! This is the day whereon nothing amongst all things, nor any name amongst all names, can profit you save through this Name which God hath made the Manifestation of His Cause and the Dayspring of His Most Excellent Titles unto all who are in the kingdom of creation. Blessed is that man that hath recognized the fragrance of the All-Merciful and been numbered with the steadfast. Your sciences shall not profit you in this day, nor your arts, nor your treasures, nor your glory. Cast them all behind your backs, and set your faces towards the Most Sublime Word through which the Scriptures and the Books and this lucid Tablet have been distinctly set forth. Cast away, O people, the things ye have composed with the pen of your idle fancies and vain imaginings. By God! The Day-Star of Knowledge hath shone forth above the horizon of certitude.

"O thou who art gone astray! If thou hast any doubt concerning Our conduct, know thou that We bear witness unto that whereunto God hath Himself borne witness ere the creation of the heavens and of the earth, that there is none other God but Him, the Almighty, the All-Bounteous. We testify that He is One in His Essence, One in His Attributes. He hath none to equal Him in the whole universe, nor any partner in all creation. He hath sent forth His Messengers, and sent down His Books, that they may announce unto His creatures the Straight Path.

"Hath the Sháh been informed, and chosen to close his eyes to thine acts? Or hath he been seized with fear at the howling of a pack of wolves who have cast the path of God behind their backs and followed in thy way without any clear proof or Book? We have heard that the provinces of Persia have been adorned with the adornment of justice. When We observed closely, however, We found them to be the dawning-places of tyranny and the dayspring of injustice. We behold justice in the clutches of tyranny. We beseech God to set it free through the power of His might and His sovereignty. He, verily, overshadoweth all that is in the heavens and on earth. To none is given the right to protest against any one concerning that which hath befallen the Cause of God. It behooveth whosoever hath set his face towards the Most Sublime Horizon to cleave tenaciously unto the cord of patience, and to put his reliance in God, the Help in Peril, the Unconstrained. O ye loved ones of God! Drink your fill from the well-spring of wisdom, and soar ye in the atmosphere of wisdom, and speak forth with wisdom and eloquence. Thus biddeth you your Lord, the Almighty, the All-Knowing.

"O heedless one! Rely not on thy glory, and thy power. Thou art even as the last trace of sunlight upon the mountain-top. Soon will it fade away as decreed by God, the All-Possessing, the Most High. Thy glory and the glory of such as are like thee have been taken away, and this verily is what hath been ordained by the One with Whom is the Mother Tablet. Where is he to be found who contended with God, and whither is gone he that gainsaid His signs, and turned aside from His sovereignty? Where are they who have slain His chosen ones and spilt the blood of His holy ones? Reflect, that haply thou mayest perceive the breaths of thine acts, O foolish doubter! Because of you the Apostle (Muḥammad) lamented, and the Chaste One (Fáṭimih) cried out, and the countries were laid waste, and darkness fell upon all regions. O concourse of divines! Because of you the people were abased, and the banner of Islám was hauled down, and its mighty throne subverted. Every time a man of discernment hath sought to hold fast unto that which would exalt Islám, ye raised a clamor, and thereby was he deterred from achieving his purpose, while the land remained fallen in clear ruin.

"O My Supreme Pen! Call Thou to remembrance the She-Serpent (Imám-Jum'ih of Iṣfahán) whose cruelty hath caused all created things to groan, and the limbs of the holy ones to quake. Thus biddeth Thee the Lord of all names, in this glorious station. The Chaste One (Fáṭimih) hath cried out by reason of thine iniquity, and yet thou dost imagine thyself to be of the family of the Apostle of God! Thus hath thy soul prompted thee, O thou who hast withdrawn thyself from God, the Lord of all that hath been and shall be. Judge thou equitably, O She-Serpent! For what crime didst thou sting the children of the Apostle of God (King of Martyrs and Beloved of Martyrs), and pillage their possessions? Hast thou denied Him Who created thee by His command 'be, and it was'? Thou hast dealt with the children of the Apostle of God as neither 'Ád hath dealt with Húd, nor Thamúd with Ṣáliḥ, nor the Jews with the Spirit of God (Jesus), the Lord of all being. Gainsayest thou the signs of thy Lord which had no sooner been sent down from the heaven of His Cause than all the books of the world bowed down before them? Meditate, that thou mayest be made aware of thine act, O heedless outcast! Ere long will the breaths of chastisement seize thee, as they seized others before thee. Wait, O thou who hast joined partners with God, the Lord of the visible and the invisible. This is the day which God hath announced through the tongue of His Apostle. Reflect, that thou mayest apprehend what the All-Merciful hath sent down in the Qur'án and in this inscribed Tablet. This is the day whereon He Who is the Dayspring of Revelation hath come with clear tokens which none can number. This is the day whereon every man endued with perception hath discovered the fragrance of the breeze of the All-Merciful in the world of creation, and every man of insight hath hastened unto the living waters of the mercy of his Lord, the King of Kings. O heedless one! The tale of the Sacrifice (Ishmael) hath been retold, and he who was to be offered up hath directed his steps towards the place of sacrifice, and returned not, by reason of that which thy hand hath wrought, O perverse hater! Didst thou imagine that martyrdom could abase this Cause? Nay, by Him Whom God hath made to be the Repository of His Revelation, if thou be of them that comprehend. Woe betide thee, O thou who hast joined partners with God, and woe betide them that have taken thee as their leader, without a clear token or a perspicuous Book. How numerous the oppressors before thee who have arisen to quench the light of God, and how many the impious who murdered and pillaged until the hearts and souls of men groaned by reason of their cruelty! The sun of justice hath been obscured, inasmuch as the embodiment of tyranny hath been stablished upon the throne of hatred, and yet the people understand not. O foolish one! Thou hast slain the children of the Apostle and pillaged their possessions. Say: Was it, in thine estimation, their possessions or themselves that denied God? Judge fairly, O ignorant one that hath been shut out as by a veil from God. Thou hast clung to tyranny, and cast away justice; whereupon all created things have lamented, and still thou art among the wayward. Thou hast put to death the aged, and plundered the young. Thinkest thou that thou wilt consume that which thine iniquity hath amassed? Nay, by Myself! Thus informeth thee He Who is cognizant of all. By God! The things thou possessest shall profit thee not, nor what thou hast laid up through thy cruelty. Unto this beareth witness thy Lord, the All-Knowing. Thou hast arisen to put out the light of this Cause; ere long will thine own fire be quenched, at His behest. He, verily, is the Lord of strength and of might. The changes and chances of the world, and the powers of the nations, cannot frustrate Him. He doeth what He pleaseth, and ordaineth what He willeth through the power of His sovereignty. Consider the she-camel. Though but a beast, yet hath the All-Merciful exalted her to so high a station that the tongues of the earth made mention of her and celebrated her praise. He, verily, overshadoweth all that is in the heavens and on earth. No God is there but Him, the Almighty, the Great. Thus have We adorned the heaven of Our Tablet with the suns of Our words. Blessed the man that hath attained thereunto, and been illumined with their light, and woe betide such as have turned aside, and denied Him, and strayed far from Him. Praised be God, the Lord of the worlds!"

O Shaykh! We have enabled thee to hear the melodies of the Nightingale of Paradise, and unveiled to thine eyes the signs which God, by His all-compelling behest, hath sent down in the Most Great Prison, that thine eye might be cheered, and thy soul be well-assured. He, verily, is the All-Bounteous, the Generous. Arise thou through the power of His testimony to serve the Cause of God, thy Lord, the God of Mercy. If thy faith be fearful, seize thou My Tablet, and preserve it in the bosom of trust. And when thou enterest into the place of resurrection, and God asketh thee by what proof thou hast believed in this Revelation, draw forth the Tablet and say: "By this Book, the holy, the mighty, the incomparable." Thereupon all will lift up their hands towards thee, and will seize the Tablet, and will press it to their eyes, and will inhale therefrom the fragrance of the utterance of God, the Lord of the worlds. Were God to torment thee for having believed in His signs in this Revelation, for what reason could He then torment such as have disbelieved in Muḥammad, the Apostle of God, and before Him in Jesus, the Son of Mary, and before Him in the One Who conversed with God (Moses), and before Him in the One Who is the Friend of God (Abraham), and as far back as the One Who was the First Manifestation, Who was created by the will of thy Lord, the Potent, the All-Encompassing. Thus have We sent down Our verses unto one before thee, and recalled them unto thee, in this day, that thou mayest understand, and be of them who are well assured. O thou who assumest the voice of knowledge! This Cause is too evident to be obscured, and too conspicuous to be concealed. It shineth as the sun in its meridian glory. None can deny it unless he be a hater and a doubter.

At this moment it behooveth us to turn unto the Desired One, and cleave unto these most sublime words: "O God, my God! Thou hast lighted the lamp of Thy Cause with the oil of wisdom; protect it from contrary winds. The lamp is Thine, and the glass is Thine, and all things in the heavens and on earth are in the grasp of Thy power. Bestow justice upon the rulers, and fairness upon the divines. Thou art the All-Powerful, Who, through the motion of Thy Pen, hast aided Thine irresistible Cause, and guided aright Thy loved ones. Thou art the Possessor of power, and the King of might. No God is there but Thee, the Strong, the Unconstrained." Say thou also: "O God, my God! I yield Thee thanks inasmuch as Thou hast made me to drink of Thy Sealed Wine from the hand of the bounty of Thy Name, the Self-Subsisting. I entreat Thee by the splendors of the Dayspring of Thy Revelation, and by the potency of Thy Most Sublime Word, and by the might of Thy Most Exalted Pen, through Whose movement the realities of all created things have been enraptured, to aid His Majesty the Sháh to render Thy Cause victorious, and to turn towards the horizon of Thy Revelation, and to set his face in the direction of the lights of Thy countenance. Assist him, O my Lord, to draw nigh unto Thee. Help him, then, with the hosts of the heavens and of earth. I implore Thee, O Thou Who art the Lord of all Names and the Maker of the heavens, by the light of Thy Cause, and by the fire of the Lote-Tree of Thy loving-kindness, to help His Majesty to reveal Thy Cause amidst Thy creatures. Open, then, before his face the doors of Thy grace, and Thy mercy, and Thy bounty. Potent art Thou to do what pleaseth Thee by Thy word: 'Be, and it is.' "

O Shaykh! We had seized the reins of authority by the power of God and His Divine might, as He alone can seize, Who is the Mighty, the Strong. None had the power to stir up mischief or sedition. Now, however, as they have failed to appreciate this loving-kindness and these bounties, they have been, and will be, afflicted with the retribution which their acts must entail. The State officials, considering the secret progress of the Extended Cord have, from every direction, incited and aided Mine adversaries. In the Great City (Constantinople) they have roused a considerable number of people to oppose this Wronged One. Things have come to such a pass that the officials in that city have acted in a manner which hath brought shame to both the government and the people. A distinguished siyyid, whose well-known integrity, acceptable conduct, and commercial reputation, were recognized by the majority of fair-minded men, and who was regarded by all as a highly honored merchant, once visited Beirut. In view of his friendship for this Wronged One they telegraphed the Persian Dragoman informing him that this siyyid, assisted by his servant, had stolen a sum of money and other things and gone to 'Akká. Their design in this matter was to dishonor this Wronged One. And yet, far be it from the people of this country to allow themselves to be deflected, by these unseemly tales, from the straight path of uprightness and truth. Briefly, they have assaulted Me from every side, and are reinforcing Mine adversaries. This Wronged One, however, beseecheth the one true God to graciously assist every one in that which beseemeth these days. Day and night I fix My gaze on these perspicuous words, and recite: "O God, my God! I beseech Thee by the sun of Thy grace, and the sea of Thy knowledge, and the heaven of Thy justice, to aid them that have denied Thee to confess, and such as have turned aside from Thee to return, and those who have calumniated Thee to be just and fair-minded. Assist them, O my Lord, to return unto Thee, and to repent before the door of Thy grace. Powerful art Thou to do what Thou willest, and in Thy grasp are the reins of all that is in the heavens and all that is on earth. Praise be unto God, the Lord of the worlds."

The time is at hand when whatsoever lieth hid in the souls and hearts of men will be disclosed. This Day is the Day whereof Luqmán spoke unto his son, the Day which the Lord of Glory announced and with which He acquainted Him Who was His Friend (Muḥammad) through these, His words—exalted be He:—"O my son! Verily, God will bring everything to light, though it were but the weight of a grain of mustard-seed, and hidden in a rock or in the heavens or in the earth; for God is Subtile, informed of all." This Day the deceitful of eye, and all that men's breasts conceal, are made known and laid bare before the throne of His Revelation. Nothing whatsoever can escape His knowledge. He heareth and seeth, and He, in truth, is the All-Hearing, the All-Seeing. How very strange that they discern not between the trustworthy and the treacherous!

Would that His Majesty the Sháh of Persia—may

God perpetuate his sovereignty—would inquire from the Consuls of the honored Persian Government who have been in this country, that he might become acquainted with the activities and behavior of this Wronged One. Briefly, they have incited a great many such as Akhtar and others, and are busying themselves in spreading calumnies. It is clear and evident that they will surround with their swords of hatred and their shafts of enmity the one whom they knew to be an outcast among men and to have been banished from one country to another. This is not the first time that such iniquity hath been perpetrated, nor the first goblet that hath been dashed to the ground, nor the first veil that hath been rent in twain in the path of God, the Lord of the worlds. This Wronged One, however, remained calm and silent in the Most Great Prison, busying Himself with His own affairs, and completely detached from all else but God. Iniquity waxed so grievous that the pens of the world are powerless to record it.

In this connection it is necessary to mention the following occurrence, that haply men may take fast hold of the cord of justice and truthfulness. Ḥájí Shaykh Muḥammad 'Alí—upon him be the glory of God, the Ever-Abiding—was a merchant of high repute, well-known unto most of the inhabitants of the Great City (Constantinople). Not long ago, when the Persian Embassy in Constantinople was secretly engaged in stirring up mischief, it was noticed that this believing and sincere soul was greatly distressed. Finally, one night he threw himself into the sea, but was rescued by some passers-by who chanced to come upon him at that moment. His act was widely commented upon and given varied interpretations by different people. Following this, one night he repaired to a mosque, and, as reported by the guardian of that place, kept vigil the whole night, and was occupied until the morning in offering, ardently and with tearful eyes, his prayers and supplications. Upon hearing him suddenly cease his devotions, the guardian went to him, and found that he had already surrendered his soul. An empty bottle was found by his side, indicating that he had poisoned himself. Briefly, the guardian, while greatly astonished, broke the news to the people. It was found out that he had left two testaments. In the first he recognized and confessed the unity of God, that His Exalted Being had neither peer nor equal, and that His Essence was exalted above all praise, all glorification and description. He also testified to the Revelation of the Prophets and the holy ones, and recognized what had been written down in the Books of God, the Lord of all men. On another page, in which he had set down a prayer, he wrote these words in conclusion: "This servant and the loved ones of God are perplexed. On the one hand the Pen of the Most High hath forbidden all men to engage in sedition, contention or conflict, and on the other that same

Pen hath sent down these most sublime words: 'Should anyone, in the presence of the Manifestation, discover an evil intention on the part of any soul, he must not oppose him, but must leave him to God.' Considering that on the one hand this binding command is clear and firmly established, and that on the other calumnies, beyond human strength to bear or endure, have been uttered, this servant hath chosen to commit this most grievous sin. I turn suppliantly unto the ocean of God's bounty and the heaven of Divine mercy, and hope that He will blot out with the pen of His grace and bounteousness the misdeeds of this servant. Though my transgressions be manifold, and unnumbered my evil-doings, yet do I cleave tenaciously to the cord of His bounty, and cling unto the hem of His generosity. God is witness, and they that are nigh unto His Threshold know full well, that this servant could not bear to hear the tales related by the perfidious. I, therefore, have committed this act. If He chastise me, He verily is to be praised for what He doeth; and if He forgive me, His behest shall be obeyed."

Ponder, now, O Shaykh, the influence of the word of God, that haply thou mayest turn from the left hand of idle fancy unto the right hand of certitude. This Wronged One hath never acted hypocritically towards any one, in the Cause of God, and hath loudly proclaimed the Word of God before the face of His creatures. Let him who wisheth turn thereunto, and let him who wisheth turn aside. If these things, however, that are so clear, so manifest and indubitable, be denied, what else can be deemed acceptable and worthy of credence in the estimation of men of insight? We beseech God—blessed and glorified be He—to forgive the aforementioned person (Ḥájí Shaykh Muḥammad-'Alí), and change his evil deeds into good ones. He, verily, is the All-Powerful, the Almighty, the All-Bounteous.

Such things have appeared in this Revelation that there is no recourse for either the exponents of science and knowledge or the manifestations of justice and equity other than to recognize them. It is incumbent upon thee, in this day, to arise with celestial power and dissipate, with the aid of knowledge, the doubts of the peoples of the world, so that all men may be sanctified, and direct their steps towards the Most Great Ocean and cleave fast unto that which God hath purposed.

Every one who hath turned aside from Me hath clung to his own idle words, and therewith voiced his objections to Him Who is the Truth. Gracious God! Such references as have been made to Divinity and Godhead by the holy ones and chosen ones of God have been made a cause for denial and repudiation. The Imám Ṣádiq hath said: "Servitude is a substance, the essence of which is Divinity." The Commander of the Faithful (Imám 'Alí) answered an Arab, who had questioned him concerning the soul, as follows: "The third is the soul which is divine and celestial. It is a divine energy, a substance, simple, and self-subsistent." And further he—peace be upon him—said: "Therefore it is the Most Sublime Essence of God, the Tree of Blessedness, the Lote-Tree beyond which there is no passing, the Garden of Repose." The Imám Ṣádiq hath said: "When our Qá'im will arise, the earth will shine with the light of her Lord." Likewise, a lengthy tradition is attributed to Abí-'Abdi'lláh—peace be upon him—in which these sublime words are found: "Thereupon will He Who is the All-Compelling— exalted and glorified be He—descend from the clouds with the angels." And in the mighty Qur'án: "What can such expect but that God should come down to them overshadowed with clouds?" And in the tradition of Mufaḍḍal it is said: "The Qá'im will lean His back against the Sanctuary, and will stretch forth His hand, and lo, it shall be snow-white but unhurt. And He shall say: 'This is the hand of God, the right hand of God, that cometh from God, at the command of God!'" In whichever manner these traditions are interpreted, in that same manner let them also interpret that which the Most Sublime Pen hath set down. The Commander of the Faithful (Imám 'Alí) hath said: "I am He Who can neither be named, nor described." And likewise He hath said: "Outwardly I am an Imám; inwardly I am the Unseen, the Unknowable." Abú-Ja'far-i-Ṭúsí hath said: "I said to

Abí 'Abdi'lláh: 'You are the Way mentioned in the Book of God, and you are the Impost, and you are the Pilgrimage.' He replied: 'O man! We are the Way mentioned in the Book of God,—exalted and glorified be He—and We are the Impost, and We are the Fast, and We are the Pilgrimage, and We are the Sacred Month, and We are the Sacred City, and We are the Kaaba of God, and We are the Qiblih of God, and We are the Face of God.'" Jábir hath said that Abú-Ja'far—peace be upon him—spoke to him as follows: "O Jábir! Give heed unto the Bayán (Exposition) and the Ma'ání (Significances)." He —peace be upon him—added: "As to the Bayán, it consisteth in thy recognition of God—glorified be He—as the One Who hath no equal, and in thy adoration of Him, and in thy refusal to join partners with Him. As to the Ma'ání, We are its meaning, and its side, and its hand, and its tongue, and its cause, and its command, and its knowledge, and its right. If We wish for something, it is God Who wisheth it, and He desireth that which We desire." Moreover, the Commander of the Faithful (Imám 'Alí)—peace be upon him—hath said: "How can I worship a Lord Whom I have not seen?" And, in another connection, he saith: "Nothing have I perceived except that I perceived God before it, God after it, or God with it."

O Shaykh! Ponder upon the things which have been mentioned, perchance thou mayest quaff the Sealed Wine through the power of the name of Him

[113]

Who is the Self-Subsisting, and obtain that which no one is capable of comprehending. Gird up the loins of endeavor, and direct thyself towards the Most Sublime Kingdom, that haply thou mayest perceive, as they descend upon Me, the breaths of Revelation and inspiration, and attain thereunto. Verily, I say: The Cause of God hath never had, nor hath it now, any peer or equal. Rend asunder the veils of idle fancies. He, in truth, will reinforce thee, and assist thee, as a token of His grace. He, verily, is the Strong, the All-Subduing, the Almighty. While there is yet time, and the blessed Lote-Tree is still calling aloud amongst men, suffer not thyself to be deprived. Place thy trust in God, and commit thine affairs unto Him, and enter then the Most Great Prison, that thou mayest hear what no ear hath ever heard, and gaze on that which no eye hath ever seen. After such an exposition, can there remain any room for doubt? Nay, by God, Who standeth over His Cause! In truth I say: On this day the blessed words "But He is the Apostle of God, and the Seal of the Prophets" have found their consummation in the verse "The day when mankind shall stand before the Lord of the worlds." Render thou thanksgiving unto God, for so great a bounty.

O Shaykh! The breezes of Revelation can never be confounded with other breezes. Now the Lote-Tree beyond which there is no passing standeth laden with countless fruits before thy face; besmirch not thyself with idle fancies, as have done the people aforetime. These utterances themselves proclaim the true nature of the Faith of God. He it is Who witnesseth unto all things. To demonstrate the truth of His Revelation He hath not been, nor is He, dependent upon any one. Well nigh a hundred volumes of luminous verses and perspicuous words have already been sent down from the heaven of the will of Him Who is the Revealer of signs, and are available unto all. It is for thee to direct thyself towards the Ultimate Goal, and the Supreme End, and the Most Sublime Pinnacle, that thou mayest hear and behold what hath been revealed by God, the Lord of the worlds.

Ponder a while upon the verses concerning the Divine Presence, which have been sent down in the Qur'án by Him Who is the Lord of the kingdom of names, perchance thou mayest discover the Straight Path, and be made an instrument for the guidance of His creatures. Such a one as thou must needs in this day arise to serve this Cause. The abasement of this Wronged One as well as thy glory shall both pass away. Strive thou, that haply thou mayest achieve a deed the fragrance of which shall never fade from the earth. Concerning the Divine Presence there hath been sent down what no denier hath been or is now able to refute or repudiate. He—blessed and exalted be He—saith: "It is God Who hath reared the heavens without pillars thou canst behold;

then mounted His throne, and imposed laws on the sun and moon: each traveleth to its appointed goal. He ordereth all things. He maketh His signs clear, that ye may have firm faith in the Presence of your Lord." He also saith: "To him who hopeth to attain the Presence of God, the set time of God will surely come. And He is the Hearer, the Knower." And further He—exalted be He—saith: "As for those who believe not in the signs of God, or that they shall ever attain His Presence, these of My mercy shall despair, and these doth a grievous chastisement await." And likewise He saith: "And they say, 'What! when we shall have lain hidden in the earth, shall we become a new creation?' Yea, they deny that they shall attain the Presence of their Lord." And likewise He saith: "They truly doubt the Presence of their Lord. He, verily, overshadoweth all things." And likewise He saith: "Verily, they who hope not to attain Our Presence, and find their satisfaction in this world's life, and rest on it, and who of Our signs are heedless—these! their abode the fire, in recompense of their deeds!" And likewise He saith: "But when Our clear signs are recited to them, they who look not forward to attain Our Presence, say, 'Bring a different Qur'án from this, or make some change in it.' Say: It is not for Me to change it as Mine own soul prompteth. I follow only what is revealed to Me: verily, I fear, if I rebel against My Lord, the punishment of a great day." And likewise He saith:

"Then gave We the Book to Moses—complete for Him who should do right, and a decision for all matters, and a guidance, and a mercy, that they might believe in the Presence of their Lord." And likewise he saith: "They are those who believe not in the signs of the Lord, or that they shall ever attain His Presence. Vain, therefore, are their works; and no weight will We allow them on the Day of Resurrection. This shall be their reward—Hell. Because they were unbelievers, and treated My signs and My Apostles with scorn." And likewise He saith: "Hath the history of Moses reached thee? When He saw a fire, and said to His family, 'Tarry ye here, for I perceive a fire; haply I may bring you a brand from it, or find at the fire a guide.' And when He came to it, He was called to, 'O Moses! Verily, I am Thy Lord; therefore pull off Thy shoes, for Thou art in the holy vale of Towa. And I have chosen Thee; hearken then to what shall be revealed. Verily, I am God, there is no God but Me. Therefore, worship Me.' " And likewise He saith: "Have they not considered within themselves that God hath not created the heavens and the earth and all that is between them but for a serious end, and for a fixed term? But truly most men believe not that they shall attain the Presence of their Lord." And likewise He saith: "What! Have they no thought that they shall be raised again for the Great Day, the Day when mankind shall stand before the Lord of the worlds?" And likewise

He saith: "We heretofore gave the Book to Moses. Have thou no doubt.as to His attaining Our Presence." And He saith: "Aye! But when the earth shall be crushed with crushing, crushing, and thy Lord shall come and the angels rank on rank." And likewise He saith: "Fain would they put out the light of God with their mouths! But though the infidels hate it, God will perfect His light." And likewise He saith: "And when Moses had fulfilled the term, and was journeying with His family, He perceived a fire on the mountain side. He said to His family: 'Wait ye, for I perceive a fire, haply I may bring you tidings from it, or a brand from the fire to warm you.' And when He came up to it, a Voice cried to Him out of the Bush from the right side of the Vale in the sacred Spot: 'O Moses, I truly am God, the Lord of the worlds!' "

In all the Divine Books the promise of the Divine Presence hath been explicitly recorded. By this Presence is meant the Presence of Him Who is the Dayspring of the signs, and the Dawning-Place of the clear tokens, and the Manifestation of the Excellent Names, and the Source of the attributes, of the true God, exalted be His glory. God in His Essence and in His own Self hath ever been unseen, inaccessible, and unknowable. By Presence, therefore, is meant the Presence of the One Who is His Vicegerent amongst men. He, moreover, hath never had, nor hath He, any peer or likeness. For were He to have any peer or likeness, how could it then be demonstrated that His being is exalted above, and His essence sanctified from, all comparison and likeness? Briefly, there hath been revealed in the Kitáb-i-Íqán (Book of Certitude) concerning the Presence and Revelation of God that which will suffice the fairminded. We beseech Him—exalted be He—to aid every one to become the essence of truthfulness, and to draw nigh unto Him. He, verily, is the Lord of strength and power. No God is there but Him, the All-Hearing, the Lord of Utterance, the Almighty, the All-Praised.

O thou who art reputed for thy learning! Bid men to do that which is praiseworthy, and be not of such as tarry. Observe thou with a keen eye. The Sun of Truth shineth resplendently, at the bidding of the Lord of the kingdom of utterance, and the King of the heaven of knowledge, above the horizon of the prison-city of 'Akká. Repudiation hath not veiled it, and ten thousand hosts arrayed against it were powerless to withhold it from shining. Thou canst excuse thyself no longer. Either thou must recognize it, or—God forbid—arise and deny all the Prophets!

Reflect, O Shaykh, upon the Shí'ih sect. How many the edifices which they reared with the hands of idle fancies and vain imaginings, and how numerous the cities which they built! At length those vain imaginings were converted into bullets and aimed

at Him Who is the Prince of the world. Not one
single soul among the leaders of that sect acknowledged Him in the Day of His Revelation! Whenever His blessed name was mentioned, all would say:
"May God hasten the joy His coming will bring!"
On the day of the Revelation of that Sun of Truth,
however, all, as hath been observed, have exclaimed,
saying: "May God hasten His chastisement!" He Who
was the Essence of being and Lord of the seen and
unseen they suspended, and committed what made
the Tablet to weep, and the Pen to groan, and the
cries of the sincere to break forth, and the tears of
the favored ones to flow.

Meditate, O Shaykh, and be fair in what thou
sayest. The followers of Shaykh-i-Aḥsá'í (Shaykh
Aḥmad) have, by the aid of God, apprehended that
which was veiled from the comprehension of others,
and of which they remained deprived. Briefly, in
every age and century differences have arisen in the
days of the manifestation of the Daysprings of Revelation, and the Dawning-Places of inspiration, and
the Repositories of Divine knowledge, differences
which have been caused and provoked by lying and
impious souls. To expatiate on this is not permissible.
Thou art thyself better acquainted and more familiar
with the idle fancies of the superstitious and the
vain imaginings of the doubters.

In this day, this Wronged One requesteth thee and
the other divines who have drunk of the cup of the

knowledge of God, and are illumined by the shining words of the Day-Star of Justice, to appoint some person, without informing any one, and despatch him to these regions, and enable him to remain a while in the island of Cyprus, and associate with Mírzá Yaḥyá, perchance he may become aware of the fundamentals of this Faith and of the source of the Divine laws and commandments.

Wert thou to ponder a while, thou wouldst bear witness unto the wisdom, and the power, and the sovereignty of God, exalted be His glory. The few who were unaware of this Cause, and had not met Us, have spoken in such a manner that all things, and those souls who are well assured, pleased, and pleasing unto God, have testified unto the imposture of these heedless ones. Wert thou now to exert thyself, the truth of this Cause would be made apparent unto mankind, and the people would be delivered from this grievous and oppressive darkness. Who else but Bahá can speak forth before the face of men, and who else but He can have the power to pronounce that which He was bidden by God, the Lord of Hosts?

This heedless one hath now clung to the practice of Rawḍih-khání (traditional lamentation for the Imám Ḥusayn). He—I swear by God—is in evident error. For it is the belief of this people that during the Revelation of the Qá'im, the Imáms—may the peace of God be upon them—have arisen from their sepulchres. This verily is the truth, and no doubt is there about it. We beseech God to bestow upon the superstitious a portion of the living waters of certitude which are streaming from the wellspring of the Most Sublime Pen, that all may attain unto that which becometh these days.

O Shaykh! While hemmed in by tribulations this Wronged One is occupied in setting down these words. On every side the flame of oppression and tyranny can be discerned. On the one hand, tidings have reached Us that Our loved ones have been arrested in the land of Ṭá (Ṭihrán) and this notwithstanding that the sun, and the moon, and the land, and the sea all testify that this people are adorned with the adornment of fidelity, and have clung and will cling to naught except that which can ensure the exaltation of the government, and the maintenance of order within the nation, and the tranquillity of the people.

O Shaykh! We have time and again stated that for a number of years We have extended Our aid unto His Majesty the Sháh. For years no untoward incident hath occurred in Persia. The reins of the stirrers of sedition among various sects were held firmly in the grasp of power. None hath transgressed his limits. By God! This people have never been, nor are they now, inclined to mischief. Their hearts are illumined with the light of the fear of God, and adorned with the adornment of His love. Their concern hath ever been and now is for the betterment of the world. Their purpose is to obliterate differences, and quench the flame of hatred and enmity, so that the whole earth may come to be viewed as one country.

On the other hand, the officials of the Persian Embassy in the Great City (Constantinople) are energetically and assiduously seeking to exterminate these wronged ones. They desire one thing, and God desireth another. Consider now what hath befallen the trusted ones of God in every land. At one time they have been accused of theft and larceny; at another they have been calumniated in a manner without parallel in this world. Answer thou fairly. What could be the results and consequences, in foreign countries, of the accusation of theft brought by the Persian Embassy against its own subjects? If this Wronged One was ashamed, it was not because of the humiliation it brought this servant, but rather because of the shame of its becoming known to the Ambassadors of foreign countries how incompetent and lacking in understanding are several eminent officials of the Persian Embassy. "Flingest thou thy calumnies into the face of Them Whom the one true God hath made the Trustees of the treasures of His seventh sphere?" Briefly, instead of seeking, as they should, through Him Who occupieth this sublime station, to attain unto the most exalted ranks, and to obtain His advice, they have exerted themselves and are striving their utmost to put out His light. However, according to what hath been reported, His Excellency the Ambassador Muʻínuʼl-Mulk, Mírzá Muḥsin Khán—may God assist him—was, at that time, absent from Constantinople. Such things have happened because it was believed that His Majesty the Sháh of Persia—may the All-Merciful assist him —was angry with them that have attained and re-volve round the Sanctuary of Wisdom. God well knoweth and testifieth that this Wronged One hath, at all times, been cleaving fast unto whatever would be conducive to the glory of both the government and the people. God, verily, is sufficient Witness.

Describing the people of Bahá, the Most Sublime Pen hath sent down these words: "These, verily, are men who if they come to cities of pure gold will consider them not; and if they meet the fairest and most comely of women will turn aside." Thus hath it been sent down by the Most Sublime Pen for the people of Bahá, on the part of Him Who is the Counsellor, the Omniscient. In the concluding passages of the Tablet to His Majesty the Emperor of Paris (Napoleon III) these exalted words have been revealed: "Exultest thou over the treasures thou dost possess, knowing they shall perish? Rejoicest thou in that thou rulest a span of earth, when the whole world, in the estimation of the people of Bahá, is worth as much as the black in the eye of a dead ant? Abandon it unto such as have set their affections upon it, and turn thou unto Him Who is the Desire of the world."

God alone—exalted be His glory—is cognizant of the things which befell this Wronged One. Every day bringeth a fresh report of stories current against Us at the Embassy in Constantinople. Gracious God! The sole aim of their machinations is to bring about the extermination of this servant. They are, however, oblivious of the fact that abasement in the path of God is My true glory. In the newspapers the following hath been recorded: "Touching the fraudulent dealings of some of the exiles of 'Akká, and the excesses committed by them against several people, etc. . . ." Unto them who are the exponents of justice and the daysprings of equity the intention of the writer is evident and his purpose clear. Briefly, he arose and inflicted upon Me divers tribulations, and treated Me with injustice and cruelty. By God! This Wronged One would not barter this place of exile for the Most Sublime Habitation. In the estimation of men of insight whatsoever befalleth in the path of God is manifest glory and a supreme attainment. Already We have said: "Glory to Thee, O my God! But for the tribulations which are sustained in Thy path, how could Thy true lovers be recognized; and were it not for the trials which are borne for love of Thee, how could the station of such as yearn for Thee be revealed?"

Such abasement hath been inflicted that each day

they spread fresh calumnies. This Wronged One, however, cleaveth to seemly patience. Would that His Majesty the Sháh of Persia would ask for a report of the things which befell Us in Constantinople, that he might become fully acquainted with the true facts. O Sháh! I adjure thee by thy Lord, the God of Mercy, to look into this matter with the eye of fairness. Is there to be found a just man who will judge in this day according to that which God hath sent down in His Book? Where is the fair-minded person who will equitably consider what hath been perpetrated against Us without any clear token or proof?

O Shaykh! Ponder the behavior of men. The inmates of the cities of knowledge and wisdom are sore perplexed asking themselves why it is that the Shí'ih sect, which regarded itself as the most learned, the most righteous, and the most pious of all the peoples of the world, hath turned aside in the Day of His Revelation, and hath shown a cruelty such as hath never been experienced. It is incumbent upon thee to reflect a while. From the inception of this sect until the present day how great hath been the number of the divines that have appeared, none of whom became cognizant of the nature of this Revelation. What could have been the cause of this waywardness? Were We to mention it, their limbs would cleave asunder. It is necessary for them to meditate, to meditate for a thousand thousand years, that haply they may attain unto a sprinkling from the ocean of knowledge, and discover the things whereof they are oblivious in this day.

I was walking in the Land of Ṭá (Ṭihrán)—the dayspring of the signs of thy Lord—when lo, I heard the lamentation of the pulpits and the voice of their supplication unto God, blessed and glorified be He. They cried out and said: "O God of the world and Lord of the nations! Thou beholdest our state and the things which have befallen us by reason of the cruelty of Thy servants. Thou hast created us and revealed us for Thy glorification and praise. Thou dost now hear what the wayward proclaim upon us in Thy days. By Thy might! Our souls are melted and our limbs are trembling. Alas, alas! Would that we had never been created and revealed by Thee!"

The hearts of them that enjoy near access to God are consumed by these words, and from them the cries of such as are devoted to Him are raised. Time and again have We, for the sake of God, admonished the distinguished divines, and summoned them unto the Most Sublime Horizon, that perchance they might, in the days of His Revelation, obtain their portion of the ocean of the utterance of Him Who is the Desire of the world, and remain not utterly deprived thereof.

In most of Our Tablets this most weighty exhortation hath been sent down from the heaven of His all-encompassing mercy. We said: "O concourse of rulers and divines! Incline your ears unto the Voice calling from the horizon of 'Akká. Verily, it aideth you to proceed aright, and draweth you nigh unto Him, and directeth your steps towards the station which God hath made the dayspring of His Revelation and the Dawning-Place of His splendors. O peoples of the world! He Who is the Most Great Name is come, on the part of the Ancient King, and hath announced unto men this Revelation which lay hid in His knowledge, and was preserved in the treasury of His protection, and was written down by the Most Sublime Pen in the Books of God, the Lord of Lords. O people of Shín (Shíráz)! Have ye forgotten My loving-kindness and My mercy that have surpassed all created things, and which proceeded from God Who layeth low the necks of men?"

In the Kitáb-i-Aqdas (Most Holy Book) the following hath been revealed: "Say: O leaders of religion! Weigh not the Book of God with such standards and sciences as are current amongst you, for the Book itself is the unerring Balance established amongst men. In this most perfect Balance whatsoever the peoples and kindreds possess must be weighed, while the measure of its weight should be tested according to its own standard, did ye but know it. The eye of My loving-kindness weepeth sore over you, inasmuch as ye have failed to recognize the One upon Whom ye have been calling in the daytime and in the night season, at even and at morn. Advance, O people, with snow-white faces and radiant hearts, unto the blest and crimson Spot, wherein the Tree beyond which there is no passing is calling: 'Verily, there is none other God beside Me, the Omnipotent Protector, the Self-Subsisting!' O ye leaders of religion in Persia! Who is the man amongst you that can rival Me in vision or insight? Where is he to be found that dareth to claim to be My equal in utterance or wisdom? No, by My Lord, the All-Merciful! All on the earth shall pass away; and this is the face of your Lord, the Almighty, the Well-Beloved. We have decreed, O people, that the highest and last end of all learning be the recognition of Him Who is the Object of all knowledge; and yet behold how ye have allowed your learning to shut you out, as by a veil, from Him Who is the Dayspring of this Light, through Whom every hidden thing hath been revealed. Say: This, verily, is the heaven in which the Mother Book is treasured, could ye but comprehend it. He it is Who hath caused the Rock to shout, and the Burning Bush to lift up its voice upon the Mount rising above the Holy Land, and proclaim: 'The Kingdom is God's, the sovereign Lord of all, the All-Powerful, the Loving!' We have not entered any school, nor read any of your dissertations. Incline your ears to the words of this unlettered One, wherewith He summoneth you unto God, the Ever-Abiding. Better is this for you than all the treasures of the earth, could ye but comprehend it. Whoso interpreteth what hath been sent down from the heaven of Revelation, and altereth its evident meaning, he, verily, is of them that have perverted the Sublime Word of God, and is of the lost ones in the Lucid Book."

Thereupon We heard the groaning of the true Faith, and said unto it: "Wherefore, O true Faith, do I hear Thee cry out in the night season, and groan in the daytime, and utter Thy lamentations at daybreak?" She made reply: "O Prince of the world that standest revealed in the Most Great Name! The heedless ones have hamstrung Thy white She-Camel, and caused Thy Crimson Ark to founder, and wished to put out Thy Light, and to veil the face of Thy Cause. Wherefore hath the voice of My lamentation been lifted up, as well as the voice of the lamentation of all created things, and yet the people are for the most part unaware." The true Faith hath laid fast hold, in this day, on the hem of Our bounty, and circleth about Our Person.

O Shaykh! Enter thou My presence, that thou mayest behold what the eye of the universe hath never beheld, and hear that which the ear of the whole creation hath never heard, that haply thou mayest free thyself from the mire of vague fancies, and set thy face towards the Most Sublime Station, wherein this Wronged One calleth aloud: "The Kingdom is God's, the Almighty, the All-Praised!" We fain would hope that through thine exertions the wings of men may be sanctified from the mire of self and desire, and be made worthy to soar in the atmosphere of God's love. Wings that are besmirched with mire can never soar. Unto this testify they who are the exponents of justice and equity, and yet the people are in evident doubt.

O Shaykh! Protests have been voiced against Us from every side—protests such as Our pen craveth pardon for setting down. Nevertheless, by reason of Our great mercy, We have replied unto them, in accordance with the understanding of men, that haply they may be delivered from the fire of negation and denial, and become illumined with the light of affirmation and acceptance. Equity is rarely to be found, and justice hath ceased to exist.

Among others, these perspicuous verses have, in answer to certain individuals, been sent down from the Kingdom of Divine knowledge: "O thou who hast set thy face towards the splendors of My Countenance! Vague fancies have encompassed the dwellers of the earth and debarred them from turning towards the Horizon of Certitude, and its brightness, and its manifestations and its lights. Vain imaginings have withheld them from Him Who is the Self-Subsisting. They speak as prompted by their own caprices, and understand not. Among them are those who have said: 'Have the verses been sent down?' Say: 'Yea, by Him Who is the Lord of the heavens!' 'Hath the Hour come?' 'Nay, more; it hath passed, by Him Who is the Revealer of clear tokens! Verily, the Inevitable is come, and He, the True One, hath appeared with proof and testimony. The Plain is disclosed, and mankind is sore vexed and fearful. Earthquakes have broken loose, and the tribes have lamented, for fear of God, the Lord of Strength, the All-Compelling.' Say: 'The stunning trumpet-blast hath been loudly raised, and the Day is God's, the One, the Unconstrained.' 'Hath the Catastrophe come to pass?' Say: 'Yea, by the Lord of Lords!' 'Is the Resurrection come?' 'Nay, more; He Who is the Self-Subsisting hath appeared with the Kingdom of His signs.' 'Seest thou men laid low?' 'Yea, by my Lord, the Exalted, the Most High!' 'Have the tree-stumps been uprooted?' 'Yea, more; the mountains have been scattered in dust; by Him the Lord of attributes!' They say: 'Where is Paradise, and where is Hell?' Say: 'The one is reunion with Me; the other thine own self, O thou who dost associate a partner with God and doubtest.' They say: 'We see not the Balance.' Say: 'Surely, by my Lord, the God of Mercy! None can see it except such as are endued with insight.' 'Have the stars fallen?' Say: 'Yea, when He Who is the Self-Subsisting dwelt in the Land of Mystery (Adrianople). Take heed, ye who are endued with discernment!' All the signs appeared when We drew forth the Hand of Power from the bosom of majesty and might. Verily, the Crier hath cried out, when the promised time came, and they that have recognized the splendors of Sinai have swooned away in the wilderness of hesitation, before the awful majesty of thy Lord, the Lord of creation. The trumpet asketh: 'Hath the Bugle been sounded?' Say: 'Yea, by the King of Revelation!, when He mounted the throne of His Name, the All-Merciful.' Darkness hath been chased away by the dawning-light of the mercy of thy Lord, the Source of all light. The breeze of the All-Merciful hath wafted, and the souls have been quickened in the tombs of their bodies. Thus hath the decree been fulfilled by God, the Mighty, the Beneficent. They that have gone astray have said: 'When were the heavens cleft asunder?' Say: 'While ye lay in the graves of way-wardness and error.' Among the heedless is he who rubbeth his eyes, and looketh to the right and to the left. Say: 'Blinded art thou. No refuge hast thou to flee to.' And among them is he who saith: 'Have men been gathered together?' Say: 'Yea, by my Lord!, whilst thou didst lie in the cradle of idle fan-cies.' And among them is he who saith: 'Hath the Book been sent down through the power of the true Faith?' Say: 'The true Faith itself is astounded. Fear ye, O ye men of understanding heart!' And among them is he who saith: 'Have I been assembled with others, blind?' Say: 'Yea, by Him that rideth upon the clouds!' Paradise is decked with mystic roses, and hell hath been made to blaze with the fire of the impious. Say: 'The light hath shone forth from the

[133]

horizon of Revelation, and the whole earth hath been illumined at the coming of Him Who is the Lord of the Day of the Covenant!' The doubters have perished, whilst he that turned, guided by the light of assurance, unto the Dayspring of Certitude hath prospered. Blessed art thou, who hast fixed thy gaze upon Me, for this Tablet which hath been sent down for thee—a Tablet which causeth the souls of men to soar. Commit it to memory, and recite it. By My life! It is a door to the mercy of thy Lord. Well is it with him that reciteth it at eventide and at dawn. We, verily, hear thy praise of this Cause, through which the mountain of knowledge was crushed, and men's feet have slipped. My glory be upon thee and upon whomsoever hath turned unto the Almighty, the All-Bounteous. The Tablet is ended, but the theme is unexhausted. Be patient, for thy Lord is patient."

These are verses We sent down previously, soon after Our arrival in the prison-city of 'Akká, and We have sent them unto thee, that thou mayest be acquainted with what their lying tongues have spoken, when Our Cause came unto them with might and sovereignty. The foundations of idle fancies have trembled, and the heaven of vain imaginings hath been cleft asunder, and yet the people are in doubt and in contention with Him. They have denied the testimony of God and His proof, after He came from the heaven of power with the kingdom of His signs. They have cast away what had been prescribed, and perpetrated what had been forbidden them in the Book. They have abandoned their God, and clung unto their desires. They truly have strayed and are in error. They read the verses and deny them. They behold the clear tokens and turn aside. They truly are lost in strange doubt.

We have admonished Our loved ones to fear God, a fear which is the fountain-head of all goodly deeds and virtues. It is the commander of the hosts of justice in the city of Bahá. Happy the man that hath entered the shadow of its luminous standard, and laid fast hold thereon. He, verily, is of the Companions of the Crimson Ark, which hath been mentioned in the Qayyúm-i-Asmá.

Say: O people of God! Adorn your temples with the adornment of trustworthiness and piety. Help, then, your Lord with the hosts of goodly deeds and a praiseworthy character. We have forbidden you dissension and conflict in My Books, and My Scriptures, and My Scrolls, and My Tablets, and have wished thereby naught else save your exaltation and advancement. Unto this testify the heavens and the stars thereof, and the sun and the radiance thereof, and the trees and the leaves thereof, and the seas and the waves thereof, and the earth and the treasures thereof. We pray God to assist His loved ones, and aid them in that which beseemeth them in this blest, this mighty, and wondrous station.

Further, in another Tablet, We have said: "O thou who hast fixed thy gaze upon My countenance! Admonish men to fear God. By God! This fear is the chief commander of the army of thy Lord. Its hosts are a praiseworthy character and goodly deeds. Through it have the cities of men's hearts been opened throughout the ages and centuries, and the standards of ascendancy and triumph raised above all other standards."

"We will now mention unto thee Trustworthiness and the station thereof in the estimation of God, thy Lord, the Lord of the Mighty Throne. One day of days We repaired unto Our Green Island. Upon Our arrival, We beheld its streams flowing, and its trees luxuriant, and the sunlight playing in their midst. Turning Our face to the right, We beheld what the pen is powerless to describe; nor can it set forth that which the eye of the Lord of Mankind witnessed in that most sanctified, that most sublime, that blest, and most exalted Spot. Turning, then, to the left We gazed on one of the Beauties of the Most Sublime Paradise, standing on a pillar of light, and calling aloud saying: 'O inmates of earth and heaven! Behold ye My beauty, and My radiance, and My revelation, and My effulgence. By God, the True One! I am Trustworthiness and the revelation thereof, and the beauty thereof. I will recompense whosoever will cleave unto Me, and recognize My rank and station, and hold fast unto My hem. I am the most great ornament of the people of Bahá, and the vesture of glory unto all who are in the kingdom of creation. I am the supreme instrument for the prosperity of the world, and the horizon of assurance unto all beings.' Thus have We sent down for thee that which will draw men nigh unto the Lord of creation."

This Wronged One hath, at all times, summoned the peoples of the world unto that which will exalt them, and draw them nigh unto God. From the Most Sublime Horizon there hath shone forth that which leaveth no room unto any one for vacillation, repudiation or denial. The wayward, however, have failed to profit therefrom; nay, it shall only increase their loss.

O Shaykh! It is incumbent upon the divines to unite with His Majesty, the Sháh—may God assist him—and to cleave day and night unto that which will exalt the station of both the government and the nation. This people are assiduously occupied in enlightening the souls of men and in rehabilitating their condition. Unto this testifieth that which hath been sent down by the Most Sublime Pen in this lucid Tablet. How often have things been simple and easy of accomplishment, and yet most men have been heedless, and busied themselves with that which wasteth their time!

One day, while in Constantinople, Kamál Páshá visited this Wronged One. Our conversation turned upon topics profitable unto man. He said that he had learned several languages. In reply We observed: "You have wasted your life. It beseemeth you and the other officials of the Government to convene a gathering and choose one of the divers languages, and likewise one of the existing scripts, or else to create a new language and a new script to be taught children in schools throughout the world. They would, in this way, be acquiring only two languages, one their own native tongue, the other the language in which all the peoples of the world would converse. Were men to take fast hold on that which hath been mentioned, the whole earth would come to be regarded as one country, and the people would be relieved and freed from the necessity of acquiring and teaching different languages." When in Our presence, he acquiesced, and even evinced great joy and complete satisfaction. We then told him to lay this matter before the officials and ministers of the Government, in order that it might be put into effect throughout the different countries. However, although he often returned to see Us after this, he never again referred to this subject, although that which had been suggested is conducive to the concord and the unity of the peoples of the world.

We fain would hope that the Persian Government will adopt it and carry it out. At present, a new language and a new script have been devised. If thou desirest, We will communicate them to thee. Our purpose is that all men may cleave unto that which will reduce unnecessary labor and exertion, so that their days may be befittingly spent and ended. God, verily, is the Helper, the Knower, the Ordainer, the Omniscient.

God willing, Persia may be adorned with, and attain unto, that whereof she hath thus far been deprived. Say: "O Sháh! Exert thyself so that all the peoples of the world may be illumined with the effulgent splendors of the sun of thy justice. The eyes of this Wronged One are turned towards naught save trustworthiness, truthfulness, purity, and all that profiteth men." Regard Him not as a traitor. Glorified art Thou, O my God, and my Master, and my Mainstay! Aid Thou His Majesty the Sháh to execute Thy laws and Thy commandments, and show forth Thy justice among Thy servants. Thou art, verily, the All-Bounteous, the Lord of grace abounding, the Almighty, the All-Powerful. The Cause of God hath come as a token of His grace. Happy are they who act; happy are they who understand; happy the man that hath clung unto the truth, detached from all that is in the heavens and all that is on earth.

O Shaykh! Seek thou the shore of the Most Great Ocean, and enter, then, the Crimson Ark which God hath ordained in the Qayyúm-i-Asmá for the people of Bahá. Verily, it passeth over land and sea. He that entereth therein is saved, and he that turneth aside perisheth. Shouldst thou enter therein and attain unto it, set thy face towards the Kaaba of God, the Help in Peril, the Self-Subsisting, and say: "O my God! I beseech Thee by Thy most glorious light, and all Thy lights are verily glorious." Thereupon, will the doors of the Kingdom be flung wide before thy face, and thou wilt behold what eyes have never beheld, and hear what ears have never heard. This Wronged One exhorteth thee as He hath exhorted thee before, and hath never had any wish for thee save that thou shouldst enter the ocean of the unity of God, the Lord of the worlds. This is the day whereon all created things cry out, and announce unto men this Revelation, through which hath appeared what was concealed and preserved in the knowledge of God, the Mighty, the All-Praised.

O Shaykh! Thou hast heard the sweet melodies of the Doves of Utterance cooing on the boughs of the Lote-Tree of knowledge. Hearken, now, unto the notes of the Birds of Wisdom upraised in the Most Sublime Paradise. They verily will acquaint thee with things of which thou wert wholly unaware. Give ear unto that which the Tongue of Might and Power hath spoken in the Books of God, the Desire of every understanding heart. At this moment a Voice was raised from the Lote-Tree beyond which there is no passing, in the heart of the Most Sublime Paradise, bidding Me relate unto thee that which hath been sent down in the Books and Tablets, and the things spoken by My Forerunner, Who laid down His life for this Great Announcement, this Straight Path. He hath said—and He, verily, speaketh the truth: "I have written down in My mention of Him these gem-like words: 'No allusion of Mine can allude unto Him, neither anything mentioned in the Bayán.'" And further, He—exalted and glorified be He—saith, concerning this most mighty Revelation, this Great Announcement: "Exalted and glorified is He above the power of any one to reveal Him except Himself, or the description of any of His creatures. I Myself am but the first servant to believe in Him and in His signs, and to partake of the sweet savors of His words from the first-fruits of the Paradise of His knowledge. Yea, by His glory! He is the Truth. There is none other God but Him. All have arisen at His bidding." Such are the words sung by the Dove of Truth on the boughs of the Divine Lote-Tree. Well is it with him that hath given ear unto its Voice, and quaffed from the oceans of Divine utterance that lie concealed in each of these words. In another connection hath the Voice of the Bayán called aloud from the loftiest branches. He saith—blessed and glorified be He: "In the year nine ye will attain unto all good." On another occasion He saith: "In the year nine ye will attain unto the Presence of God." These melodies, uttered by the Birds of the cities of Knowledge, conform with that which hath

[141]

been sent down by the All-Merciful in the Qur'án. Blessed are the men of insight; blessed they that attain thereunto.

O Shaykh! I swear by God! The River of Mercy floweth, and the Ocean of Utterance surgeth, and the Sun of Revelation shineth forth resplendent. With a detached heart, and a dilated breast, and an utterly truthful tongue, recite thou these sublime words that have been revealed by My Forerunner—the Primal Point. He saith—glorified be His utterance—addressing his honor, 'Azím: "This, verily, is the thing We promised thee, ere the moment We answered thy call. Wait thou until nine will have elapsed from the time of the Bayán. Then exclaim: 'Blessed, therefore, be God, the most excellent of Makers!' Say: This, verily, is an Announcement which none except God hath comprehended. Ye, however, will be unaware on that day." In the year nine this Most Great Revelation arose and shone forth brightly above the horizon of the Will of God. None can deny it save he who is heedless and doubteth. We pray God to aid His servants to return unto Him, and beg forgiveness for the things they committed in this vain life. He, verily, is the Forgiving, the Pardoner, the All-Merciful. In another connection He saith: "I am the first servant to believe in Him, and in His signs." In like manner, in the Persian Bayán, He saith: "He, verily, is the One Who, under all conditions, proclaimeth: 'I, in very truth, am

God!' " and so on—blessed and glorified be He. That which is meant by Divinity and Godhead hath previously been stated. We have in truth rent the veils asunder and disclosed that which will draw men nigh unto God, Who layeth low the necks of men. Happy the man that hath attained unto justice and equity in this Grace that hath encompassed all that is in the heavens and all that is on earth, as bidden by God, the Lord of the worlds.

O Shaykh! Hearken unto the melodies of the Gospel with the ear of fairness. He saith—glorified be His utterance—prophesying the things that are to come: "But of that Day and Hour knoweth no man, no, not the angels of heaven, nor the Son, but the Father." By Father in this connection is meant God—exalted be His glory. He, verily, is the True Educator, and the Spiritual Teacher.

Joel saith: "For the Day of the Lord is great and very terrible; and who can abide it?" Firstly, in the sublime utterance set forth in the Gospel He saith that none is aware of the time of the Revelation, that none knoweth it except God, the All-Knowing, Who is cognizant of all. Secondly, He setteth forth the greatness of the Revelation. Likewise, in the Qur'án He saith: "Of what ask they of one another? Of the Great Announcement." This is the Announcement, the greatness of which hath been mentioned in most of the Books of old and of more recent times. This is the Announcement that hath caused the limbs of mankind to quake, except such as God, the Protector, the Helper, the Succorer, hath willed to exempt. Men have indeed with their own eyes witnessed how all men and all things have been thrown into confusion and been sore perplexed, save those whom God hath chosen to exempt.

O Shaykh! Great is the Cause, and great the Announcement! Patiently and calmly ponder thou upon the resplendent signs and the sublime words, and all that hath been revealed in these days, that haply thou mayest fathom the mysteries that are hid in the Books, and mayest strive to guide His servants. Hearken with thine inner ear unto the Voice of Jeremiah, Who saith: "Oh, for great is that Day, and it hath no equal." Wert thou to observe with the eye of fairness, thou wouldst perceive the greatness of the Day. Incline thine ear unto the Voice of this All-Knowing Counsellor, and suffer not thyself to be deprived of the mercy that hath surpassed all created things, visible and invisible. Lend an ear unto the song of David. He saith: "Who will bring me into the Strong City?" The Strong City is 'Akká, which hath been named the Most Great Prison, and which possesseth a fortress and mighty ramparts.

O Shaykh! Peruse that which Isaiah hath spoken in His Book. He saith: "Get thee up into the high mountain, O Zion, that bringest good tidings; lift up Thy Voice with strength, O Jerusalem, that bringest good tidings. Lift it up, be not afraid; say unto the cities of Judah: 'Behold your God! Behold the Lord God will come with strong hand, and His arm shall rule for Him.' " This Day all the signs have appeared. A Great City hath descended from heaven, and Zion trembleth and exulteth with joy at the Revelation of God, for it hath heard the Voice of God on every side. This Day Jerusalem hath attained unto a new Evangel, for in the stead of the sycamore standeth the cedar. Jerusalem is the place of pilgrimage for all the peoples of the world, and hath been named the Holy City. Together with Zion and Palestine, they are all included within these regions. Wherefore, hath it been said: "Blessed is the man that hath migrated to 'Akká."

Amos saith: "The Lord will roar from Zion, and utter His Voice from Jerusalem; and the habitations of the shepherds shall mourn, and the top of Carmel shall wither." Carmel, in the Book of God, hath been designated as the Hill of God, and His Vineyard. It is here that, by the grace of the Lord of Revelation, the Tabernacle of Glory hath been raised. Happy are they that attain thereunto; happy they that set their faces towards it. And likewise He saith: "Our God will come, and He will not be silent."

O Shaykh! Reflect upon these words addressed by Him Who is the Desire of the world to Amos. He saith: "Prepare to meet thy God, O Israel, for, lo, He that formeth the mountains and createth the wind, and declareth unto man what is his thought, that maketh the morning darkness, and treadeth upon the high places of the earth, the Lord, the God of Hosts, is His name." He saith that He maketh the morning darkness. By this is meant that if, at the time of the Manifestation of Him Who conversed on Sinai anyone were to regard himself as the true morn, he will, through the might and power of God, be turned into darkness. He truly is the false dawn, though believing himself to be the true one. Woe unto him, and woe unto such as follow him without a clear token from God, the Lord of the worlds.

Isaiah saith: "The Lord alone shall be exalted in that Day." Concerning the greatness of the Revelation He saith: "Enter into the rock, and hide thee in the dust, for fear of the Lord, and for the glory of His majesty." And in another connection He saith: "The wilderness and the solitary place shall be glad for them; and the desert shall rejoice, and blossom as the rose. It shall blossom abundantly, and rejoice even with joy and singing: the glory of Lebanon shall be given unto it, the splendor of Carmel and Sharon, they shall see the glory of the Lord, and the splendor of our God."

These passages stand in need of no commentary. They are shining and manifest as the sun, and glowing and luminous as light itself. Every fair-minded person is led, by the fragrance of these words, unto the garden of understanding, and attaineth unto that from which most men are veiled and debarred. Say:

Fear God, O people, and follow not the doubts of such as shout aloud, who have broken the Covenant of God and His Testament, and denied His mercy that hath preceded all that are in the heavens and all that are on earth.

And likewise, He saith: "Say to them that are of a fearful heart: be strong, fear not, behold your God." This blessed verse is a proof of the greatness of the Revelation, and of the greatness of the Cause, inasmuch as the blast of the trumpet must needs spread confusion throughout the world, and fear and trembling amongst all men. Well is it with him who hath been illumined with the light of trust and detachment. The tribulations of that Day will not hinder or alarm him. Thus hath the Tongue of Utterance spoken, as bidden by Him Who is the All-Merciful. He, verily, is the Strong, the All-Powerful, the All-Subduing, the Almighty. It is now incumbent upon them who are endowed with a hearing ear and a seeing eye to ponder these sublime words, in each of which the oceans of inner meaning and explanation are hidden, that haply the words uttered by Him Who is the Lord of Revelation may enable His servants to attain, with the utmost joy and radiance, unto the Supreme Goal and Most Sublime Summit—the dawning-place of this Voice.

O Shaykh! Wert thou to perceive, be it less than a needle's eye, the breaths of Mine utterance, thou wouldst abandon the world and all that is therein, and wouldst set thy face towards the lights of the countenance of the Desired One. Briefly, in the sayings of Him Who is the Spirit (Jesus) unnumbered significances lie concealed. Unto many things did He refer, but as He found none possessed of a hearing ear or a seeing eye He chose to conceal most of these things. Even as He saith: "But ye cannot bear them now." That Dawning-Place of Revelation saith that on that Day He Who is the Promised One will reveal the things which are to come. Accordingly in the Kitáb-i-Aqdas, and in the Tablets to the Kings, and in the Lawḥ-i-Ra'ís, and in the Lawḥ-i-Fu'ád, most of the things which have come to pass on this earth have been announced and prophesied by the Most Sublime Pen.

In the Kitáb-i-Aqdas the following hath been revealed: "O Land of Ṭá (Ṭihrán)! Let nothing grieve thee, for God hath chosen thee to be the source of the joy of all mankind. He shall, if it be His Will, bless thy throne with one who will rule with justice, who will gather together the flock of God which the wolves have scattered. Such a ruler will, with joy and gladness, turn his face towards, and extend his favors unto, the people of Bahá. He indeed is accounted in the sight of God, as a jewel among men. Upon him rest forever the glory of God, and the glory of all that dwell in the kingdom of His revelation." These verses were revealed previously. Now, however, the following verse hath been sent down:

"O God, my God! Bahá beseecheth Thee and imploreth Thee, by the lights of Thy countenance and the billows of the ocean of Thy Revelation, and the effulgent splendors of the Sun of Thine utterance, to aid the Sháh to be fair and equitable. If it be Thy wish, bless Thou, through him, the throne of authority and sovereignty. Potent art Thou to do what pleaseth Thee. There is none other God but Thee, Who hearest, Who art ready to answer." "Rejoice with great joy, O Land of Ṭá (Ṭihrán), for God hath made thee the dayspring of His light, inasmuch as within thee was born the Manifestation of His glory. Be thou glad for this name that hath been conferred upon thee—a name through which the Day-Star of grace hath shed its splendor, through which both earth and heaven have been illumined. Ere long will the state of affairs within thee be changed, and the reins of power fall into the hands of the people. Verily, thy Lord is the All-Knowing. His authority embraceth all things. Rest thou assured in the gracious favor of Thy Lord. The eye of His loving-kindness shall everlastingly be directed towards thee. The day is approaching when thy agitation will have been transmuted into peace and quiet calm. Thus hath it been decreed in the Wondrous Book."

And likewise, in the Lawḥ-i-Fu'ád, and in the Tablet of the King of Paris (Napoleon III), and in other Tablets, there hath been revealed that which will lead every fair-minded person to testify unto the power, and the majesty, and the wisdom of God—exalted be His glory. Were men to observe with the eye of justice, they would be made aware of the secret of this blessed verse: "Neither is there a thing green or sere, but it is noted in a distinct writing," and would comprehend it. On this day, however, men's repudiation of the truth hath prevented them from understanding what hath been sent down in truth by Him Who is the Revealer, the Ancient of Days. Gracious God! Perspicuous signs have appeared on every side, and yet men are, for the most part, deprived of the privilege of beholding and of comprehending them. We beseech God to bestow His aid, that all men may recognize the pearls that lie hid within the shells of the Most Great Ocean, and exclaim: "Praised be Thou, O God of the world!"

O concourse of the fair-minded! Observe and reflect upon the billows of the ocean of the utterance and knowledge of God, so that ye may testify with your inner and outer tongues that with Him is the knowledge of all that is in the Book. Nothing escapeth His knowledge. He, verily, hath manifested that which was hidden, when He, upon His return, mounted the throne of the Bayán. All that hath been sent down hath and will come to pass, word for word, upon earth. No possibility is left for anyone either to turn aside or protest. As fairness, however, is disgraced and concealed, most men speak as prompted by their own idle fancies.

O God, my God! Debar not Thy servants from turning their faces towards the light of certitude, that hath dawned above the horizon of Thy will, and suffer them not to be deprived, O my God, of the oceans of Thy signs. They, O my Lord, are Thy servants in Thy cities, and Thy slaves in Thy lands. If Thou hast not mercy upon them, who, then, will show them mercy? Take Thou, O my God, the hands of such as have been drowned in the sea of idle fancies, and deliver them by Thy power and Thy sovereignty. Save them, then, with the arms of Thy might. Powerful art Thou to do what Thou willest, and in Thy right hand are the reins of all that is in the heavens and all that is on earth.

In like manner, the Primal Point saith: "Behold ye Him with His own eyes. Were ye to behold Him with the eyes of another, ye would never recognize and know Him." This referreth to naught else except this Most Great Revelation. Well is it with them that judge fairly. And likewise, He saith: "The year-old germ that holdeth within itself the potentialities of the Revelation that is to come is endowed with a potency superior to the combined forces of the whole of the Bayán." These glad-tidings of the Bayán and of the Books of former times have been repeatedly mentioned under divers names in numerous books, that perchance men might judge equitably that which hath arisen and shone forth above the horizon of the will of God, the Lord of the Mighty Throne.

O Shaykh! Tell the people of the Bayán: "Ponder ye these blessed words. He saith: 'The whole of the Bayán is only a leaf amongst the leaves of His Paradise.' Be fair, O people, and be not of such as are accounted as lost in the Book of God, the Lord of the worlds." The blessed Lote-Tree standeth, in this day, before thy face, laden with heavenly, with new and wondrous fruits. Gaze on it, detached from all else save it. Thus hath the Tongue of might and power spoken at this Spot which God hath adorned with the footsteps of His Most Great Name and Mighty Announcement.

And likewise, He saith: "Ere nine will have elapsed from the inception of this Cause, the realities of the created things will not be made manifest. All that thou hast as yet seen is but the stage from the moist germ until We clothed it with flesh. Be patient, until thou beholdest a new creation. Say: 'Blessed, therefore, be God, the most excellent of Makers!' " And likewise, He hath said regarding the power of this Revelation: "Lawful is it for Him Whom God will make manifest to reject him who is greatest on earth, inasmuch as such a one is but a creature in His grasp, and all things adore Him. After Hín (68) a Cause shall be given unto you which ye shall come to know."

And also He saith: "Know thou with absolute certainty, and through the firmly established and most irrevocable decree, that He—exalted be His glory, and magnified be His might, and sanctified be His holiness, and glorified be His grandeur, and lauded be His ways, maketh each thing to be known through its own self; who then can know Him through any one except Himself?" And further, He saith—exalted and glorified be He: "Beware, beware lest, in the days of His Revelation, the Váḥid of the Bayán (eighteen Letters of the Living) shut thee not out as by a veil from Him, inasmuch as this Váḥid is but a creature in His sight. And beware, beware that the words sent down in the Bayán shut thee not out as by a veil from Him." And again, He—exalted be He—saith: "Look not upon Him with any eye except His own. For whosoever looketh upon Him with His eye, will recognize Him; otherwise he will be veiled from Him. Shouldst thou seek God and His Presence, seek thou Him and gaze upon Him." And likewise, He saith: "Better is it for thee to recite but one of the verses of Him Whom God shall make manifest than to set down the whole of the Bayán, for on that Day that one verse can save thee, whereas the entire Bayán cannot save thee."

Say: O people of the Bayán! Be fair, be fair; and again, be fair, be fair. Be ye not of them who have made mention of the Manifestation of the Cause of God in the daytime and in the night season, and

[153]

who, when He, through His grace, appeared, and when the Horizon of Revelation was illumined, pronounced against Him such a judgment as hath provoked the lamentations of the inmates of the Kingdom and of the Realm of Glory, and of such as have circled about the will of God, the All-Knowing, the All-Wise.

Meditate upon these sublime words. He saith: "I, verily, am a believer in Him, and in His Faith, and in His Book, and in His Testimonies, and in His Ways, and in all that proceedeth from Him concerning them. I glory in My kinship with Him, and pride Myself on My belief in Him." And likewise, He saith: "O congregation of the Bayán and all who are therein! Recognize ye the limits imposed upon you, for such a One as the Point of the Bayán Himself hath believed in Him Whom God shall make manifest, before all things were created. Therein, verily, do I glory before all who are in the kingdom of heaven and earth." By God! All the atoms of the universe groan and lament at the cruelty perpetrated by the froward among the people of the Bayán. Whither are gone they who are endued with insight and hearing? We beseech God—blessed and glorified be He—to summon them and exhort them unto that which will profit them, and withhold them from that which will harm them. He, in truth, is the Strong, the All-Subduing, the Almighty.

And likewise, He saith: "Suffer not yourselves to

be shut out as by a veil from God after He hath
revealed Himself. For all that hath been exalted in
the Bayán is but as a ring upon My hand, and I
Myself am, verily, but a ring upon the hand of Him
Whom God shall make manifest—glorified be His
mention! He turneth it as He pleaseth, for whatsoever He pleaseth, and through whatsoever He
pleaseth. He, verily, is the Help in Peril, the Most
High." And likewise, He saith: "Were He to make of
every one on earth a Prophet, all would, in very truth,
be accounted as Prophets in the sight of God." And
likewise, He saith: "In the day of the revelation of
Him Whom God shall make manifest all that dwell
on earth will be equal in His estimation. Whomsoever
He ordaineth as a Prophet, he, verily, hath been a
Prophet from the beginning that hath no beginning,
and will thus remain until the end that hath no end,
inasmuch as this is an act of God. And whosoever
is made a Vicegerent by Him, shall be a Vicegerent
in all the worlds, for this is an act of God. For the
will of God can in no wise be revealed except through
His will, nor His wish be manifested save through His
wish. He, verily, is the All-Conquering, the All-
Powerful, the All-Highest."

Briefly, in every instance He hath stated that which
is conducive to the conversion, the advancement, the
exaltation, and the guidance of men. A few unfair
ones, however, have become a veil, and an insur-
mountable barrier, and debarred the people from

turning towards the lights of His Countenance. We pray God to cast them out by His sovereignty, and seize on them with His seizing power. He, verily, is the Lord of Strength, the Mighty, the All-Wise.

And likewise, He saith: "He—glorified be His mention—resembleth the sun. Were unnumbered mirrors to be placed before it, each would, according to its capacity, reflect the splendor of that sun, and were none to be placed before it, it would still continue to rise and set, and the mirrors alone would be veiled from its light. I, verily, have not fallen short of My duty to admonish that people, and to devise means whereby they may turn towards God, their Lord, and believe in God, their Creator. If, on the day of His Revelation, all that are on earth bear Him allegiance, Mine inmost being will rejoice, inasmuch as all will have attained the summit of their existence, and will have been brought face to face with their Beloved, and will have recognized, to the fullest extent attainable in the world of being, the splendor of Him Who is the Desire of their hearts. If not, My soul will indeed be saddened. I truly have nurtured all things for this purpose. How, then, can anyone be veiled from Him? For this have I called upon God, and will continue to call upon Him. He, verily, is nigh, ready to answer."

And likewise, He saith: "They will even refuse unto that Tree, which is neither of the East nor of the West, the name believer, for were they so to name

Him, they would fail to sadden Him." Hath thine ear, O world, heard with what helplessness these words were revealed from the dayspring of the will of Him Who is the Dawning-Place of all names? He saith: "I have educated all men, that they may recognize this Revelation, and yet the people of the Bayán refuse to concede even the name believer to that blessed Tree that belongeth neither to the East nor to the West." Alas, alas, for the things which have befallen Me! By God! There befell Me at the hands of him whom I have nurtured (Mírzá Yaḥyá), by day and by night, what hath caused the Holy Spirit, and the dwellers of the Tabernacle of the Grandeur of God, the Lord of this wondrous Day, to lament.

Likewise, refuting certain disbelievers, He saith: "For none knoweth the time of the Revelation except God. Whenever it appeareth, all must acknowledge the Point of Truth, and render thanks unto God." They that have turned aside from Me have spoken even as the followers of John (the Baptist) spoke. For they, too, protested against Him Who was the Spirit (Jesus) saying: "The dispensation of John hath not yet ended; wherefore hast thou come?" Now, too, they that have repudiated Us, though they have never known Us and have been at all times ignorant of the fundamentals of this Cause, knowing not from Whom it proceeded or what it signifieth, have spoken that which hath made all created things to sigh and lament. By My life! The mute can never confront the One Who incarnateth in Himself the kingdom of utterance. Fear God, O people, and peruse, then, that which hath been sent down with truth in the eighth Chapter of the sixth Váhid of the Bayán, and be not of such as have turned aside. He, likewise, hath commanded: "Once every nineteen days this Chapter should be read, that haply they may not be veiled, in the time of the revelation of Him Whom God shall make manifest, by considerations foreign to the verses, which have been, and are still, the weightiest of all proofs and testimonies."

John, son of Zacharias, said what My Forerunner hath said: "Saying, repent ye, for the Kingdom of heaven is at hand. I indeed baptize you with water unto repentance, but He that cometh after Me is mightier than I, Whose shoes I am not worthy to bear." Wherefore, hath My Forerunner, as a sign of submissiveness and humility, said: "The whole of the Bayán is only a leaf amongst the leaves of His Paradise." And likewise, He saith: "I am the first to adore Him, and pride Myself on My kinship with Him." And yet, O men, the people of the Bayán have acted in a manner that Dhi'l-Jawshan, and Ibn-i-Anas and Asbahí have sought and still seek refuge with God against such deeds. This Wronged One hath, in the face of all religions, busied Himself day and night with the things that are conducive unto the exaltation of the Cause of God, whereas those men have clung unto that which is the cause of humiliation and injury.

And likewise, He saith: "Recognize Him by His verses. The greater your neglect in seeking to know Him, the more grievously will ye be veiled in fire." O ye among the people of the Bayán that have turned aside from Me! Ponder upon these most sublime words, that have proceeded from the wellspring of the utterance of Him Who is the Point of Knowledge. Hearken ye, at this moment, unto these words. He saith: "On that Day, the Day-Star of Truth will address the people of the Bayán and will recite this Súrih of the Qur'án: 'Say: O ye unbelievers! I worship not that which ye worship, and ye do not worship that which I worship. I shall never worship that which ye worship, neither will ye worship that which I worship. To you be your religion, to Me My religion.'" Gracious God! Notwithstanding these lucid statements, and these shining and luminous tokens all are occupied with their vain imaginings, and are unaware of, and veiled from, the Desired One. O ye that have gone astray! Awake from the sleep of heedlessness, and give ear unto these words of My Forerunner. He saith: "The tree of affirmation, by turning aside from Him, is accounted as the tree of denial, and the tree of denial, by turning towards Him, is accounted as the tree of affirmation." And likewise, He saith: "Should anyone lay claim unto a

Revelation, and fail to produce any proof, do not protest, and sadden Him not." Briefly, this Wronged One hath, night and day, been uttering the words: "Say: O ye unbelievers!", that haply this may be the means of awakening the people, and may adorn them with the adornment of fairness.

And now, meditate upon these words, which diffuse the breath of despair, in His sorrowful invocation unto God, the Lord of the worlds. He saith: "Glorified art Thou, O My God! Bear Thou witness that, through this Book, I have covenanted with all created things concerning the Mission of Him Whom Thou shalt make manifest, ere the covenant concerning Mine own Mission had been established. Sufficient witness art Thou and they that have believed in Thy signs. Thou, verily, sufficest Me. In Thee have I placed My trust, and Thou, verily, takest count of all things."

In another connection He saith: "O Sun-like Mirrors! Look ye upon the Sun of Truth. Ye, verily, depend upon it, were ye to perceive it. Ye are all as fishes, moving in the waters of the sea, veiling yourselves therefrom, and yet asking what it is on which ye depend." And likewise, He saith: "I complain unto thee, O Mirror of My generosity, against all the other Mirrors. All look upon Me through their own colors." These words were sent down from the Source of the Revelation of the All-Bounteous, and were addressed to Siyyid Javád, known as Karbilá'í.

God testifieth, and the world beareth Me witness that this Siyyid stood by this Wronged One, and even wrote a detailed refutation against them that turned aside from Me. Two communications, moreover, in which he hath borne witness unto the Revelation of the True One, and in which the evidences of his turning away from all else but Him, are clear and manifest, have been sent by Us to Ḥaydar-'Alí. The handwriting of the Siyyid is unmistakable, and is known unto everyone. Our purpose in doing this was that perchance they that have denied Us might attain unto the living waters of acknowledgment, and such as have turned aside be illumined with the light of conversion. God is My witness that this Wronged One hath had no purpose except to convey the Word of God. Blessed are the fair-minded, and woe betide them that have turned aside. They that have turned away from Me have schemed many a time, and acted deceitfully in divers ways. They have, on one occasion, secured a picture of this Siyyid, and pasted it on a sheet with that of others, surmounted by the portrait of Mírzá Yaḥyá. Briefly, they have seized upon every means in order to repudiate the True One. Say: "The True One is come evident as the shining sun; O pity that He should have come into the city of the blind!" The afore-mentioned Siyyid admonished the deniers, and summoned them unto the Most Sublime Horizon, but failed to impress these stones that can take no imprint. Concerning

him they have said things against which he sought
refuge with God—exalted be His glory. The supplications which he hath sent to this Holy Court are now
in Our possession. Happy are the fair-minded.

Ponder now upon the complaint of the Primal
Point against the Mirrors, that haply men may be
awakened, and may turn from the left hand of idle
fancies and imaginings unto the right hand of faith
and certitude, and may be made cognizant of that
wherefrom they are veiled. It is indeed for the purpose of recognizing this Most Great Cause that they
have come out of the world of non-existence into the
world of being. And likewise He saith: "Consecrate
Thou, O my God, the whole of this Tree unto Him,
that from it may be revealed all the fruits created by
God within it for Him through Whom God hath
willed to reveal all that He pleaseth. By Thy glory!
I have not wished that this Tree should ever bear
any branch, leaf, or fruit that would fail to bow
down before Him, on the day of His Revelation, or
refuse to laud Thee through Him, as beseemeth the
glory of His all-glorious Revelation, and the sublimity of His most sublime Concealment. And shouldst
Thou behold, O my God, any branch, leaf, or fruit
upon Me that hath failed to bow down before Him,
on the day of His Revelation, cut it off, O My God,
from that Tree, for it is not of Me, nor shall it return
unto Me."

O people of the Bayán! I swear by God! This

Wronged One hath had no other intention except to manifest the Cause He was commissioned to reveal. Were ye to incline your inner ears unto Him, ye would hear from every limb and member and vein and even from every single hair of this Wronged One that which would stir and enrapture the Concourse on high and the world of creation.

O Hádí! The blind fanaticism of former times hath withheld the hapless creatures from the Straight Path. Meditate on the S͟hí'ih sect. For twelve hundred years they have cried "O Qá'im!", until in the end all pronounced the sentence of His death, and caused Him to suffer martyrdom, notwithstanding their belief in, and their acceptance and acknowledgment of, the True One—exalted be His glory—and of the Seal of the Prophets, and of the Chosen Ones. It is now necessary to reflect a while, that haply that which hath come between the True One and His creatures may be discovered, and the deeds which have been the cause of protest and denial be made known.

O Hádí! We have heard the moaning of the pulpits which, as attested by all, the divines of the age of this Revelation have ascended, and from which they have cursed the True One, and caused such things to befall Him Who is the Essence of Being and His companions as neither the eye nor the ear of the world hath seen or heard. Thou hast now summoned, and art still summoning the people, claiming to be His vicegerent and mirror, despite thine ignorance of this Cause as a result of thy not having been in Our company.

Every one of this people well knoweth that Siyyid Muḥammad was but one of Our servants. In the days when, as requested by the Imperial Ottoman Government, We proceeded to their Capital, he accompanied Us. Subsequently, he committed that which —I swear by God—hath caused the Pen of the Most High to weep and His Tablet to groan. We, therefore, cast him out; whereupon, he joined Mírzá Yaḥyá, and did what no tyrant hath ever done. We abandoned him, and said unto him: "Begone, O heedless one!" After these words had been uttered, he joined the order of the Mawlavís, and remained in their company until the time when We were summoned to depart.

O Hádí! Suffer not thyself to become the instrument for the dissemination of new superstitions, and refuse to set up once again a sect similar to that of the Shí'ihs. Reflect how great the amount of blood which hath been spilt. Thou amongst others, who hast laid claim to knowledge, and likewise the Shí'ih divines, have, one and all, in the first and ensuing years, cursed the True One, and decreed that His most holy blood be shed. Fear God, O Hádí! Be not willing that men be again afflicted with the vain imaginings of former times. Fear God, and be not of them that act unjustly. In these days We have heard that thou hast striven to lay hands on and destroy every copy of the Bayán. This Wronged One requesteth thee to renounce, for the sake of God, this intention. Thine intelligence and judgment have never excelled, nor do they now excel, the intelligence and judgment of Him Who is the Prince of the World. God testifieth and beareth Me witness that this Wronged One hath not perused the Bayán, nor been acquainted with its contents. This much, however, is known and is clear and indubitable that He hath ordained the Book of the Bayán to be the foundation of His works. Fear God, and meddle not in matters which far transcend thee. For twelve hundred years they that resemble thee have afflicted the hapless Shí'ihs in the pit of vain fancies and idle imaginings. Finally, there appeared, on the Day of Judgment things against which the oppressors of old have sought refuge with the True One.

Apprehend now the cry of Him Who is the Point as raised by His utterance. He supplicateth God that if there should appear from this Tree—which is His blessed Self—any fruit, or leaf, or branch that would fail to believe in Him, God should cut it off forthwith. And likewise, He saith: "Should any one make a statement, and fail to support it by any proof, reject him not." And yet, now, though supported by a hundred books, thou hast rejected Him and rejoicest therein!

Again I repeat, and plead with thee to carefully

scrutinize that which hath been revealed. The breezes of utterance in this Revelation are not to be compared with those of former ages. This Wronged One hath been perpetually afflicted, and found no place of safety in which He could peruse either the writings of the Most Exalted One (the Báb) or those of any one else. About two months after Our arrival in 'Iráq, following the command of His Majesty the Sháh of Persia—may God assist him—Mírzá Yaḥyá joined Us. We said unto him: "In accordance with the Royal command We have been sent unto this place. It is advisable for thee to remain in Persia. We will send Our brother, Mírzá Músá, to some other place. As your names have not been mentioned in the Royal decree, you can arise and render some service." Subsequently, this Wronged One departed from Baghdád, and for two years withdrew from the world. Upon Our return, We found that he had not left, and had postponed his departure. This Wronged One was greatly saddened. God testifieth and beareth Us witness that We have, at all times, been busied with the propagation of this Cause. Neither chains nor bonds, stocks nor imprisonment, have succeeded in withholding Us from revealing Our Self. In that land We forbad all mischief, and all unseemly and unholy deeds. Day and night We sent forth Our Tablets in every direction. We had no other purpose except to edify the souls of men, and to exalt the blessed Word.

We especially appointed certain ones to collect the writings of the Primal Point. When this was accomplished, We summoned Mírzá Yaḥyá and Mírzá Vahháb-i-Khurásání, known as Mírzá Javád, to meet in a certain place. Conforming with Our instructions, they completed the task of transcribing two copies of the works of the Primal Point. I swear by God! This Wronged One, by reason of His constant association with men, hath not looked at these books, nor gazed with outward eyes on these writings. When We departed, these writings were in the possession of these two persons. It was agreed that Mírzá Yaḥyá should be entrusted with them, and proceed to Persia, and disseminate them throughout that land. This Wronged One proceeded, at the request of the Ministers of the Ottoman Government to their capital. When We arrived in Mosul, We found that Mírzá Yaḥyá had left before Us for that city, and was awaiting Us there. Briefly, the books and writings were left in Baghdád, while he himself proceeded to Constantinople and joined these servants. God beareth now witness unto the things which have touched this Wronged One, for after We had so arduously striven, he (Mírzá Yaḥyá) abandoned the writings and joined the exiles. This Wronged One was, for a long period, overwhelmed by infinite sorrows until such time when, in pursuance of measures of which none but the one true God is aware, We despatched the writings unto another place and another country, owing to the fact that in 'Iráq all documents must every month be carefully examined, lest they rot and perish. God, however, preserved them and sent them unto a place which He had previously ordained. He, verily, is the Protector, the Succorer.

Wherever this Wronged One went Mírzá Yaḥyá followed Him. Thou art thyself a witness and well knowest that whatever hath been said is the truth. The Siyyid of Iṣfáhán, however, surreptitiously duped him. They committed that which caused the greatest consternation. Would that thou wouldst inquire from the officials of the government concerning the conduct of Mírzá Yaḥyá in that land. Aside from all this, I adjure thee by God, the One, the Incomparable, the Lord of Strength, the Most Powerful, to carefully look into the communications addressed in his name to the Primal Point, that thou mayest behold the evidences of Him Who is the Truth as clear as the sun. Likewise, there proceeded from the words of the Point of the Bayán—may the souls of all else but Him be sacrificed for His sake—that which no veil can obscure, and which neither the veils of glory nor the veils interposed by such as have gone astray can hide. The veils have, verily, been rent asunder by the finger of the will of thy Lord, the Strong, the All-Subduing, the All-Powerful. Yea, desperate is the state of such as have calumniated Me and envied Me. Not long ago it was stated that thou hadst ascribed the authorship of the Kitáb-i-Íqán and of other Tablets unto others. I swear by God! This is a grievous injustice. Others are incapable of apprehending their meaning, how much more of revealing them!

Ḥasan-i-Mázindaráni was the bearer of seventy Tablets. Upon his death, these were not delivered unto those for whom they were intended, but were entrusted to one of the sisters of this Wronged One, who, for no reason whatever, had turned aside from Me. God knoweth what befell His Tablets. This sister had never lived with Us. I swear by the Sun of Truth that after these things had happened she never saw Mírzá Yaḥyá, and remained unaware of Our Cause, for in those days she had been estranged from Us. She lived in one quarter, and this Wronged One in another. As a token, however, of Our loving-kindness, our affection and mercy, We, a few days prior to Our departure, visited her and her mother, that haply she might quaff from the living waters of faith, and attain unto that which would draw her nigh unto God, in this day. God well knoweth and beareth Me witness, and she herself testifieth, that I had no thought whatsoever except this. Finally, she —God be praised—attained unto this through His grace, and was adorned with the adornment of love. After We were exiled and had departed from 'Iráq to Constantinople, however, news of her ceased to reach Us. Subsequent to Our separation in the Land of Ṭá (Ṭihrán), We ceased to meet Mírzá Riḍá-

Qulí, Our brother, and no special news reached Us concerning her. In the early days we all lived in one house, which later on was sold at auction, for a negligible sum, and the two brothers, Farmán-Farmá and Ḥisámu's-Salṭanih, purchased it and divided it between themselves. After this occurred, We separated from Our brother. He established his residence close to the entrance of Masjid-i-S͟háh, whilst We lived near the Gate of S͟himírán. Thereafter, however, that sister displayed toward Us, for no reason whatever, a hostile attitude. This Wronged One held His peace under all conditions. However, Our late brother Mírzá Muḥammad-Ḥasan's daughter—upon him be the glory of God and His peace and His mercy —who had been betrothed to the Most Great Branch ('Abdu'l-Bahá) was taken by the sister of this Wronged One from Núr to her own house, and from there sent unto another place. Some of Our companions and friends in various places complained against this, as it was a very grievous act, and was disapproved by all the loved ones of God. How strange that Our sister should have taken her to her own house, and then arranged for her to be sent elsewhere! In spite of this, this Wronged One remained, and still remaineth, calm and silent. A word, however, was said in order to tranquilize Our loved ones. God testifieth and beareth Me witness that whatever hath been said was the truth, and was spoken with sincerity. None of Our loved ones, whether in these regions or in that country, could believe Our sister capable of an act so contrary to decency, affection and friendship. After such a thing had occurred, they, recognizing that the way had been barred, conducted themselves in a manner well-known unto thyself and others. It must be evident, therefore, how intense was the grief which this act inflicted upon this Wronged One. Later on, she threw in her lot with Mírzá Yaḥyá. Conflicting reports concerning her are now reaching Us, nor is it clear what she is saying or doing. We beseech God—blessed and glorified be He—to cause her to turn unto Him, and aid her to repent before the door of His grace. He, verily, is the Mighty, the Forgiving; and He is, in truth, the All-Powerful, the Pardoner.

In another connection He, likewise, saith: "Were He to appear this very moment, I would be the first to adore Him, and the first to bow down before Him." Be fair, O people! The purpose of the Most Exalted One (the Báb) was to insure that the proximity of the Revelation should not withhold men from the Divine and everlasting Law, even as the companions of John (the Baptist) were prevented from acknowledging Him Who is the Spirit (Jesus). Time and again He hath said: "Suffer not the Bayán and all that hath been revealed therein to withhold you from that Essence of Being and Lord of the visible and invisible." Should any one, considering this binding injunction, cling unto the Bayán, such a

[171]

one hath, verily, passed out of the shadow of the blessed and exalted Tree. Be fair, O people, and be not of the heedless.

And likewise, He saith: "Let not names shut you out as by a veil from Him Who is their Lord, even the name of Prophet, for such a name is but a creation of His utterance." And likewise, He, in the seventh chapter of the second Váḥid, saith: "O people of the Bayán! Act not as the people of the Qur'án have acted, for if ye do so, the fruits of your night will come to naught." And further, He saith—glorified be His mention: "If thou attainest unto His Revelation, and obeyest Him, thou wilt have revealed the fruit of the Bayán; if not, thou art unworthy of mention before God. Take pity upon thyself. If thou aidest not Him Who is the Manifestation of the Lordship of God, be not, then, a cause of sadness unto Him." And further He saith—magnified be His station: "If thou attainest not unto the Presence of God, grieve not, then, the Sign of God. Ye will renounce that which can profit them that acknowledge the Bayán, if ye renounce that which can harm Him. I know, however, that ye will refuse to do so."

O Hádí! Methinks it is by reason of these indubitable utterances that thou hast determined to blot out the Bayán. Give ear unto the voice of this Wronged One, and renounce this oppression that hath made the pillars of the Bayán to tremble. I have been neither in Chihríq nor in Mákú. At the present time statements have been circulated among thy disciples identical with those made by the Shí'ihs who have said that the Qur'án is unfinished. These people also contend that this Bayán is not the original one. The copy in the handwriting of Siyyid Ḥusayn is extant, as is also the copy in the handwriting of Mírzá Aḥmad.

Regardest thou as one wronged he who in this world was never dealt a single blow, and who was continually surrounded by five of the handmaidens of God? And imputest thou unto the True One, Who, from His earliest years until the present day, hath been in the hands of His enemies, and been tormented with the worst afflictions in the world, such charges as the Jews did not ascribe unto Christ? Hearken unto the voice of this Wronged One, and be not of them that are in utter loss.

And, likewise, He saith: "How many the fires which God converteth into light through Him Whom God shall make manifest; and how numerous the lights which are turned into fire through Him! I behold His appearance even as the sun in the midmost heaven, and the disappearance of all even as that of the stars of the night by day." Hast thou ears, O world, wherewith to hear the voice of the True One, and to judge equitably this Revelation Which, as soon as it appeared, Sinai exclaimed: "He that discoursed upon Me is come with evident signs and resplendent tokens, in spite of every heedless one that hath gone far astray, and of every lying calumniator, who hath wished to quench the light of God with his calumnies, and blot out the signs of God through his malice. They, verily, are of such as have acted unjustly in the Book of God, the Lord of the worlds."

And likewise, He saith: "The Bayán is from beginning to end the repository of all of His attributes, and the treasury of both His fire and His light." Great God! The soul is carried away by the fragrance of this utterance, inasmuch as He declareth, with infinite sadness, that which He perceiveth. Likewise, He saith to the Letter of the Living, Mullá Báqir—upon him be the glory of God and His loving-kindness: "Haply thou mayest in eight years, in the day of His Revelation, attain unto His Presence."

Know thou, O Hádí, and be of them that hearken. Judge thou equitably. The companions of God and the Testimonies of Him Who is the Truth have, for the most part, suffered martyrdom. Thou, however, art still alive. How is it that thou hast been spared? I swear by God! It is because of thy denial, whereas the martyrdom of the blessed souls was due to their confession. Every just and fair-minded person will bear witness unto this, inasmuch as the cause and motive of both are clear and evident as the sun.

And likewise He addresseth Dayyán, who was wronged and suffered martyrdom, saying: "Thou shalt recognize thy worth through the words of Him Whom God shall make manifest." He, likewise, hath pronounced him to be the third Letter to believe in Him Whom God shall make manifest, through these words: "O thou who art the third Letter to believe in Him Whom God shall make manifest!" And likewise He saith: "Should God, however, be willing, He will make thee known through the words of Him Whom God shall make manifest." Dayyán, who, according to the words of Him Who is the Point—may the souls of all else but Him be sacrificed for His sake—is the repository of the trust of the one true God—exalted be His glory—and the treasury of the pearls of His knowledge, was made by them to suffer so cruel a martyrdom that the Concourse on high wept and lamented. He it is whom He (the Báb) had taught the hidden and preserved knowledge and entrusted him therewith, through His words: "O thou who art named Dayyán! This is a hidden and preserved Knowledge. We have entrusted it unto thee, and brought it to thee, as a mark of honor from God, inasmuch as the eye of thine heart is pure. Thou wilt appreciate its value, and wilt cherish its excellence. God, verily, hath deigned to bestow upon the Point of the Bayán a hidden and preserved Knowledge, the like of which God hath not sent down prior to this Revelation. More precious is it than any other knowledge in the estimation of God—glorified be He! He, verily, hath made it His testimony, even as He hath made the verses to be His testimony." This oppressed one, who was the repository of the knowledge of God, together with Mírzá 'Alí-Akbar, one of the relatives of the Primal Point—upon him be the glory of God and His mercy—and Abu'l-Qásim-i-Káshí and several others suffered martyrdom through the decree pronounced by Mírzá Yaḥyá.

O Hádí! His book which he hath entitled "Mustayqíz" is in thy possession. Read it. Although thou hast seen the book, peruse it again, that haply thou mayest obtain for thyself a lofty seat beneath the canopy of truth.

In like manner, Siyyid Ibráhím, concerning whom these words have flowed from the Pen of the Primal Point—magnified be His utterance: "O thou who art mentioned as My friend in My scriptures, and as My remembrance in My books, next to My scriptures, and as My name in the Bayán"—such a one, together with Dayyán, hath been surnamed by him (Mírzá Yaḥyá) Father of Iniquities and Father of Calamities. Judge thou fairly, how grievous hath been the plight of these oppressed ones, and this notwithstanding that one of them was occupied in serving him, whilst the other was his guest. Briefly, I swear by God, the deeds he committed were such that Our Pen is ashamed to recount.

Reflect a while upon the dishonor inflicted upon the Primal Point. Consider what hath happened. When this Wronged One, after a retirement of two years during which He wandered through the deserts and mountains, returned to Baghdád, as a result of the intervention of a few, who for a long time had sought Him in the wilderness, a certain Mírzá Muḥammad-'Alí of Rasht came to see Him, and related, before a large gathering of people, that which had been done, affecting the honor of the Báb, which hath truly overwhelmed all lands with sorrow. Great God! How could they have countenanced this most grievous betrayal? Briefly, We beseech God to aid the perpetrator of this deed to repent, and return unto Him. He, verily, is the Helper, the All-Wise.

As to Dayyán—upon him be the glory of God and His mercy—he attained Our presence in accordance with that which had been revealed by the pen of the Primal Point. We pray God to aid the heedless to turn unto Him, and such as have turned aside to direct themselves towards Him, and them that have denied Him to acknowledge this Cause, which, no sooner did it appear than all created things proclaimed: "He that was hidden in the Treasury of Knowledge, and inscribed by the Pen of the Most High in His Books, and His Scriptures, and His Scrolls, and His Tablets, is come!"

In this connection it hath been deemed necessary to mention such traditions as have been recorded regarding the blessed and honored city of 'Akká, that haply thou mayest, O Hádí, seek a path unto the Truth, and a road leading unto God.

In the name of God, the Compassionate, the Merciful.

The following hath been recorded concerning the

merits of 'Akká, and of the sea, and of 'Aynu'l-Baqar (The Spring of the Cow) which is in 'Akká:

'Abdu'l-'Azíz, son of 'Abdu'-Salám, hath related unto us that the Prophet—may the blessings of God and His salutations be upon him—hath said: " 'Akká is a city in Syria to which God hath shown His special mercy."

Ibn-i-Mas'úd—may God be pleased with him—hath stated: "The Prophet—may the blessings of God and His salutations be upon Him—hath said: 'Of all shores the best is the shore of Askelon, and 'Akká is, verily, better than Askelon, and the merit of 'Akká above that of Askelon and all other shores is as the merit of Muḥammad above that of all other Prophets. I bring you tidings of a city betwixt two mountains in Syria, in the middle of a meadow, which is called 'Akká. Verily, he that entereth therein, longing for it and eager to visit it, God will forgive his sins, both of the past and of the future. And he that departeth from it, other than as a pilgrim, God will not bless his departure. In it is a spring called the Spring of the Cow. Whoso drinketh a draught therefrom, God will fill his heart with light, and will protect him from the most great terror on the Day of Resurrection.' "

Anas, son of Málik—may God be pleased with him—hath said: "The Apostle of God—may the blessings of God and His salutations be upon Him—hath said: 'By the shore of the sea is a city, suspended beneath the Throne, and named 'Akká. He that dwelleth therein, firm and expecting a reward from God—exalted be He—God will write down for him, until the Day of Resurrection, the recompense of such as have been patient, and have stood up, and knelt down, and prostrated themselves, before Him.'"

And He—may the blessings of God and His salutations be upon Him—hath said: "I announce unto you a city, on the shores of the sea, white, whose whiteness is pleasing unto God—exalted be He! It is called 'Akká. He that hath been bitten by one of its fleas is better, in the estimation of God, than he who hath received a grievous blow in the path of God. And he that raiseth therein the call to prayer, his voice will be lifted up unto Paradise. And he that remaineth therein for seven days in the face of the enemy, God will gather him with Khiḍr—peace be upon Him—and God will protect him from the most great terror on the Day of Resurrection." And He—may the blessings of God,—exalted be He—and His salutations be upon Him—hath said: "There are kings and princes in Paradise. The poor of 'Akká are the kings of Paradise and the princes thereof. A month in 'Akká is better than a thousand years elsewhere."

The Apostle of God—may the blessings of God and His salutations be upon Him—is reported to have said: "Blessed the man that hath visited 'Akká, and blessed he that hath visited the visitor of 'Akká.

Blessed the one that hath drunk from the Spring of the Cow and washed in its waters, for the black-eyed damsels quaff the camphor in Paradise, which hath come from the Spring of the Cow, and from the Spring of Salván (Siloam), and the Well of Zamzam. Well is it with him that hath drunk from these springs, and washed in their waters, for God hath forbidden the fire of hell to touch him and his body on the Day of Resurrection."

The Prophet—may the blessings of God and His salutations be upon Him—is stated to have said: "In 'Akká are works of supererogation and acts which are beneficial, which God vouchsafed specially unto whomsoever He pleaseth. And he that saith in 'Akká: 'Glorified be God, and praise be unto God, and there is none other God but God, and most great is God, and there is no power nor strength except in God, the Exalted, the Mighty,' God will write down for him a thousand good deeds, and blot out from him a thousand evil deeds, and will uplift him a thousand grades in Paradise, and will forgive him his transgressions. And whoso saith in 'Akká: 'I beg forgiveness of God,' God will forgive all his trespasses. And he that remembereth God in 'Akká at morn and at eventide, in the night-season and at dawn, is better in the sight of God than he who beareth swords, spears and arms in the path of God—exalted be He!"

The Apostle of God—may the blessings of God and His salutations be upon Him—hath also said: "He that looketh upon the sea at eventide, and saith: 'God is Most Great!' at sunset, God will forgive his sins, though they be heaped as piles of sand. And he that counteth forty waves, while repeating: 'God is Most Great!'—exalted be He—God will forgive his sins, both past and future."

The Apostle of God—may the blessings of God and His salutations be upon Him—hath said: "He that looketh upon the sea a full night is better than he who passeth two whole months betwixt the Rukn and the Maqám. And he that hath been brought up on the shores of the sea is better than he that hath been brought up elsewhere. And he that lieth on the shore is as he that standeth elsewhere."

Verily, the Apostle of God—may the blessings of God, exalted be He, and His salutations be upon Him—hath spoken the truth.

GLOSSARY

'ABÁ-BASÍR
> Son of a Zanján martyr and himself decapitated for his faith in that city.

ABHÁ PEN
> The Pen of the Most Glorious; that is, the power of the Holy Spirit manifested through the Prophet's writings.

'ABDU'L-'AZÍZ
> son of

'ABDU'L-SALÁM
> A famous Muslim ecclesiastic of the Sunní sect.

ABÍ-ABDI'LLÁH
> Arabic term used in reference to Imám Jaafar Sadiq, the sixth Shí'ih Imám. (83-148 A. H.)

ABÚ-'ALÍ SÍNÁ
> (980-1037 A. D.) or Avicenna. An Arab physician and philosopher born in Persia, known in the West as the Hippocrates and the Aristotle of the Arabs.

ABÚ-DHAR
> Abú-Dhar Ghifárí, an illiterate shepherd who became an esteemed disciple of Muḥammad.

ABÚ-JA'FAR-I-ṬÚSÍ
 AND
JÁBIR
> Two Muslims who like Mufaḍḍal handed down traditions from Imám Sadiq.

ABU'L-QÁSIM-I-KÁSHÍ
> A learned Bábí from Káshán who was murdered in Baghdád by the followers of Mírzá Yaḥyá.

ABÚ-NAṢR
> Abú-Naṣr Farabi, Persian philosopher and writer who lived about the 4th Century, A. H.

'ÁD

A powerful Arabian tribe, destroyed, like <u>Th</u>amúd, for its idolatry.

A<u>KH</u>TAR

'The Star': A Persian reformist newspaper published in Constantinople and influenced by the Azalís.

'AKKÁ

The prison city to which Bahá'u'lláh was finally exiled. He arrived there August 31, 1868.

A<u>SH</u>RAF

Áqá Mírzá A<u>sh</u>raf of Ábádih martyred in Iṣfahán, October, 1888.

ASKELON

A coast town in Southern Palestine. (Judges 14, 19)

(The) ASSEMBLY

That is, the Assembly of the representatives of the people; the Parliament.

'AYNU'L-BAQAR

An ancient spring in 'Akká.

'AẒÍM

A believer to whom the Báb revealed the name and the advent of Bahá'u'lláh. (*God Passes By* p. 28)

BÁB

The Herald of the Faith (1819-1850).

BÁBÍS

Followers of the Báb.

BADÍ'

("Wonderful") Áqá Buzurg of <u>Kh</u>urásán, bearer of the Tablet to the <u>Sh</u>áh (See *God Passes By* p. 199).

BALÁL
'SÍN' AND 'SHÍN'

The Ethiopian slave who was one of the very early converts to Islám. The Prophet gave him the task of calling the Faithful to prayer, and he became the first Mu'a<u>dhdh</u>in of Islám. As he stammered and mispro-

nounced the Arabic letter 'Shín' as 'Sín', he could not
give the call correctly, but the perfection of his heart
atoned for the fault of his tongue.

BAYÁN

The chief doctrinal work of the Founder of the Bábí
Dispensation.

BOOK OF FÁṬIMIH

The book revealed by Gabriel for Fáṭimih as consolation
after her Father's death and believed by Shí'ih Islám to
be in the Qá'im's possession. Identified with *Hidden
Words*.

CARMEL

The mountain in Israel where Bahá'u'lláh pitched His
tent and where the Shrine of the Báb is situated.

CRIMSON ARK

Each of the past Dispensations was referred to as an
"Ark." This refers to the Cause of Bahá'u'lláh.

CRIMSON BOOK

Bahá'u'lláh's Book of the Covenant. See *God Passes By*,
p. 238.

DAYYÁN

Title given by the Báb to Asadu'lláh of Khoy, a devoted
and distinguished believer. Was the third to recognize
Bahá'u'lláh's true station before His Declaration. Murdered in Baghdád by the followers of Mírzá Yaḥyá. (See
Dawnbreakers p. 303.)

DHI'L-JAWSHAN

An Arabian term meaning "clad in armor" applied to
Mullá 'Abdu'lláh the arch-killer of Imám Ḥusayn.

FARMÁN-FARMÁ

Title of Prince Firaydún Mírzá, the son of Prince 'Abbás
Mírzá, and brother of Muḥammad Sháh.

FIRST LEAF OF PARADISE

Quotation is from Bahá'u'lláh's Tablet "Words of Paradise" which has eleven numbered sections, each called a "leaf."

HÁDÍ
(Same as Mírzá Hádí)

HÁJÍ MUHAMMAD-RIDÁ
A highly respected Bahá'í of 'Ishqábád, martyred 1889.

HÁJÍ NASÍR
(of Qazvín) A merchant; full name Hájí Muhammad-Nasír; martyred at Rasht in 1300 A.H. (1882–83).

HÁJÍ SHAYKH MUHAMMAD 'ALÍ
A Bahá'í merchant from Qazvín, Persia, known as Nabíl Ibn-i-Nabíl; he lived in Istanbul from 1882 and committed suicide in that city on the 9th of Rajab 1307 (March 1, 1890).

SIYYID JAVÁD known as KARBILÁ'Í
Brought up in Karbilá, a disciple of Kázim Rashti's, and a friend of the Báb's great uncle, he met the Báb as a child and later through Mullá 'Alí Bastammi became a Bábí. He recognized Bahá'u'lláh before His Declaration, in Baghdád, and was known because of his sanctity as 'Siyyih-i-Núr'. He passed away in Kirmán, Persia.

HÁMÁN
Chief Minister of Pharaoh.

HASAN AND HUSAYN
Two brothers, honored and wealthy citizens of Isfahán, Siyyids, who were martyred as Bahá'ís at the instance of the Imám-Jum'ih of that city.

HASAN-I-MÁZINDARÁNÍ
Full name, Muhammad Hasan, a believer from the ancestral province of Bahá'u'lláh. He is a son of Mírzá Zaynu'l-'Ábidín, a paternal uncle of Bahá'u'lláh.

HAYDAR-'ALÍ
A devoted Bahá'í who, under Bahá'u'lláh and then

'Abdu'l-Bahá travelled widely in the service of the Cause and suffered much persecution. Died in Haifa, 1920, A.D. Author of the interesting narrative Bahjatus Sudour.

ḤILL AND ḤARAM

Ḥaram means 'sanctuary'. It refers to two areas near the Kaaba in which blood revenge was forbidden, and also to four months in the Arabic Calendar to which the same prohibition applied.

Ḥill means the unprotected area and the unprotected months.

The quotation from the poem here made (p. 17) means "the judge has condemned me to death both in Ḥaram and Ḥill".

ḤISÁMU'S-SALṬANIH

Title of Prince Murad Mírzá, grandson of Fatḥ-'Alí Sháh.

HÚD

A prophet sent to the tribe of 'ÁD, which was descended from Shem and was highly civilized. He summoned the people to the worship of One God, but was rejected. (Qur'án 7, 63-70 etc.)

ḤUSAYN

(Son of 'Alí) The third Imám (A.H. 61)

IBN-I-ANAS AND AṢBAHÍ

Two Arab zealots who directly took part in the murder of Imám Ḥusayn.

IBN-I-MAS'ÚD

'Abdulláh Ibn-i-Mas'úd, one of the early Arab Muslims at the time of Muḥammad.

IMÁM-JUM'IH OF IṢFAHÁN

Mír Muḥammad Ḥusayn, "the She-Serpent" (successor in this post to his brother Mír Siyyid Muḥammad who befriended the Báb—see *Dawn-Breakers*). He, with "the

Wolf," Shaykh Muḥammad Báqir, persecuted the Bahá'ís and brought about the death of Mírzá Muḥammad Ḥasan and Mírzá Muḥammad Ḥusayn (The King and the Beloved of Martyrs), who were decapitated together.

IMÁMS

Title of the twelve Shí'ih successors of Muḥammad.

IṢFAHÁN

An important city in central Persia.

KAABA

Literally, "a cube." The cube-like building in the center of the Mosque at Mecca, which contains the Black Stone.

KAMÁL PÁSHÁ

One of the Turkish dignitaries at the Court of Sulṭán 'Abdu'l-'Azíz.

KÁẒIM

Mullá Káẓim martyred in Iṣfahán. (See *Traveller's Narrative*, p. 400 note).

KHIḌR

Name of a legendary immortal saint. 'See *Qur'án* 18.62 note).

KHUṬBIY-I-ṬUTUNJÍYIH

Title of a sermon delivered by Imám 'Alí.

KITÁB-I-AQDAS

The Most Holy Book, the chief work of Bahá'u'lláh containing His Law and constituting the Charter of His New World. (1873).

KITÁB-I-ÍQÁN

The chief religious work of Bahá'u'lláh, revealed in Baghdád, 1862.

LAVÁSSÁN

A rural district lying to the east of Ṭihrán.

LAWḤ-I-FU'ÁD

A Tablet revealed by Bahá'u'lláh and addressed to Shaykh

Kázim-i-Samandar, in which reference is made to Fu'ád Páshá, after his death.

LAWḤ-I-RA'ÍS
Bahá'u'lláh's Tablet to the Grand Vizir 'Alí Páshá.

LESSER PEACE
The outward Peace which the nations will establish by their own efforts. Distinguished from The Most Great Peace.

LUQMÁN
A famous legendary figure noted for his wisdom. (See *Qur'án*, Súrih 31.)

MA'ÁNÍ
A reference to the Imáms as the repositories of the inner meanings of the Word of God.

MASJID-I-SHÁH
A great Mosque in Ṭihrán built by Fatḥ-'Alí Sháh.

MÁZINDARÁN
A province in northern Persia.

MÍRZÁ AḤMAD
Alias, Mullá 'Abdu'l-Karím of Qasvín, a devoted follower of the Báb and of Bahá'u'lláh and amanuensis of the Báb, who before His death sent through him His gifts and effects to Bahá'u'lláh.

MÍRZÁ 'ALÍ-AKBAR
A cousin (paternal) of the Báb and intimate friend of Dayyán. Murdered by the followers of Mírzá Yaḥyá.

MÍRZÁ HÁDÍ DAWLAT-ÁBÁDÍ
A noted divine from Iṣfahán who became a prominent follower of Mírzá Yaḥyá, later identified as his successor.

MÍRZÁ ḤUSAYN KHÁN, MUSHÍRU'D-DAWLIH
The Persian Ambassador at the Sublime Porte through whose influence Bahá'u'lláh was transferred from

Baghdád to Constantinople. *(God Passes By,* pp. 146 and 159).

MÍRZÁ MÚSÁ

A faithful brother of Bahá'u'lláh.

MÍRZÁ MUṢṬAFÁ

(of Naráq) One of the followers of the Báb who was executed in Tabríz. (See *Memorials of the Faithful,* pp. 148–50.)

MÍRZÁ ṚIDÁ-QULÍ

One of Bahá'u'lláh's brothers who could not recognize His station.

MÍRZÁ ṢAFÁ

Ḥájí Mírzá Ḥasan-i-Safá, an accomplice of Mírzá Ḥusayn Khán, in active hostility towards Bahá'u'lláh in Constantinople.

MÍRZÁ VAHHÁB-I-KHURÁSÁNÍ

Also known as Mírzá Javád, a prominent early believer who lived during the ministry of the Báb and Bahá'u'lláh.

MÍRZÁ YAḤYÁ

Younger half-brother of Bahá'u'lláh and His implacable enemy.

THE MOSQUE OF AQṢÁ

The name by which the Temple of Solomon in Jerusalem is referred to in the Qur'án.

MUFAḌḌAL

A devoted follower of Imám Sadiq, who has handed down many Muslim traditions from the AMAM.

MULLÁ 'ALÍ JÁN

A believer of Mázindarán: martyred in Ṭihrán. *(God Passes By,* p. 201)

MULLÁ BÁQIR

A native of Tabríz and a man of great learning, became a Letter of the Living. Was with Bahá'u'lláh in Núr,

Mázindarán and Badasht. Outlived all other Letters of
the Living.

NAJAF-'ALÍ

One of the 44 survivors of Zanján who were brought
to Ṭihrán and all of them executed save Najaf 'Alí, on
whom an officer took pity. But some years later he was
arrested again and beheaded. (See *God Passes By*, p. 178)

NAYRÍZ

A town in southern Persia, near Shíráz.

NÍYÁVARÁN

A village in which there is a royal residence.

PEOPLE OF BAHÁ

Followers of Bahá'u'lláh.

PRINCE SHUJÁ'U'D-DAWLIH

A Persian Prince attached to the Embassy at Istanbul
during reign of Sulṭán 'Abdu'l-'Azíz.

QÁ'IM

Lit. 'He Who shall arise.' The Promised One of Islám.

QÁRÚN

A cousin of Moses, who having believed in Moses, turned
against Him and with his fellow-rebels was destroyed by
the wrath of God. (See Numbers Ch. 16).

QAYYÚM-I-ASMÁ

Explanation of the "Súrih of Joseph": the first work
written by the Báb.

RASHT

A city in the Province of Gílán in northern Persia.

ṢÁD-I-IṢFAHÁNÍ

Refers to Ṣadru'l-'Ulamá of Iṣfahán, a follower of Mírzá
Yaḥyá.

SADRAH

Reference to the Sadratu'l-Muntahá or the Burning
Bush: 'Him Who taught it,' i.e., God Himself.

[191]

SADRATU'L-MUNTAHÁ

The name of a tree planted by the Arabs in ancient times at the end of a road to serve as a guide. As a symbol, a Manifestation of God.

ṢÁLIḤ

An Arabian prophet of later date than Húd, who gave a similar summons. He, too, was cast out by the people.

SALVÁN (SILOAM)

A spring in Mecca.

SARDÁR 'AZÍZ KHÁN

He was present with the Sháh's troops attacking Bábís at Zanján. (See *Traveller's Narrative*, p. 181 note.) During his tenure as governor of Tabríz several believers were executed in that city.

SHAYKH

"The Son of the Wolf," Shaykh Muḥammad Taqí, known as Aqa Najafi, a priest of Iṣfahán whose father had caused the death of the King of Martyrs and the Beloved of the Martyrs.

SHAYKH-I-AḤSÁ'Í

Shaykh Aḥmad, precursor of the Báb.

SHÍ'IH

One of the two great sects of Islám, which is dominant in Persia.

SHIMÍRÁN (gate of)

A district in the northern section of Ṭihrán.

SINAI

The mountain where the Law was revealed by God to Moses.

SIYYID (OF FINDIRÍSK)

A noted Persian poet and thinker better known as Mír-Abu'l Qásim Findiriski, who lived in the 16th Century, A.D.

SIYYID ASHRAF-I-ZANJÁNÍ

Martyred with 'Abá Nazir (See *God Passes By*, p. 199 and *Gleanings from the Writings of Bahá'u'lláh*, p. 135)

SIYYID IBRÁHÍM

Surnamed 'Khalíl' by the Báb; a deeply trusted disciple of the Báb from the earliest days. Later in Baghdád recognized the true station of Bahá'u'lláh, Who protected him against Yahyá's designs.

SIYYID ISMÁ'ÍL

A believer from the time of the Báb, who sacrificed his life for love of Bahá'u'lláh, and was given the title of 'Zabih'.

SIYYID MUHAMMAD

'The Anti-Christ of the Bahá'í Revelation' who instigated the villainies of Mírzá Yahyá.

SÚRATU'L-HAYKAL

A Tablet of Bahá'u'lláh, at the end of which followed The Tablets to the Kings, the whole being written in the shape of a five-pointed star, the symbol of man.

SÚRIH OF TAWHÍD

The name of the first Súrih of the Qur'án; in which the oneness of God is explained.

TABARSÍ

A shrine lying 14 miles southeast of Bárfurúsh, where Quddús Husayn and many leading Bábís suffered martyrdom.

THAMÚD

An ancient idolatrous tribe of Arabs, who dwelt in caves. (Qur'án, 7.71, 9.71).

TIHRÁN

The capital city of Persia and birthplace of Bahá'u'lláh.

TOWA

A holy vale in Sinai. (Qur'án 20; 10, 11, Exod. 3; I Kgs. 198.)

ZAMZAM (well of)

A well in Mecca regarded by the Muslims as sacred.

ZANJÁN

A town in western Persia, the scene of the martyrdom of 1800 Bábís led by Mullá Muḥammad 'Alí, surnamed Ḥujjat.

—Prepared by George Townshend (with the help of Bahá'í scholars in Persia)

INDEX

INDEX

INDEX